GOODBYE, MOM

Also by Arnie Singer:

The Outsider's Guide to Orthodox Judaism

Deep Waters: Insights into the Five Books of Moses (Torah) and the Jewish Festivals

GOODBYE, MOM

A MEMOIR OF PRAYER, JEWISH MOURNING AND HEALING

ARNIE SINGER

Citron Publishing, New York

ISBN 978-0-9830285-0-5

Library of Congress Control Number: 2010914036

Library of Congress Subject Headings:

Mourning Customs
Jewish Mourning Customs
Shivah
Consolation (Judaism)
Bereavement--Religious aspects—Judaism
Death --Religious aspects --Judaism.

Contact the Author at:
arnie.singer@gmail.com
www.arniesinger.com
212-663-9550

To my beloved mother,

Jeane Singer

Yehudit Bat Elimelech, Z"L

May her soul be elevated and her memory be a blessing for her children and grandchildren.

In a real dark night of the soul it is always three o'clock in

the morning, day after day.

F. SCOTT FITZGERALD

"Though I walk through the valley of the shadow of death,

I will fear no evil for You are with me."

PSALM 23

"Many are the intentions in a person's mind, but the

Lord's plan prevails."

PROVERBS 19

CONTENTS

Introduction

Almost everyone will, at some point, experience the death of a loved one and the grief and mourning that follows. It is painful, physically and psychologically taxing, and life altering. There are dozens of guide books that explain the many laws and customs related to Jewish mourning but they are mostly references that are too difficult or dry to be comfortably read cover to cover. After experiencing my mother's death and spending a year mourning for her I decided to write a book that would serve not only as a guide to Jewish mourning customs but as a source of inspiration and spiritual guidance.

In *Goodbye, Mom: A Memoir of Prayer, Jewish Mourning and Healing,* I describe my final moments with my mother, how I helped ease her journey to the next world, and how I dealt with my grief after her passing. I also explain the important role that prayer played in my struggle to help Mom live and in my attempt to honor her memory and heal my broken heart.

This book is divided into two parts. Part 1 is about life, hope, prayer, and miracles. Part 2 is about death, mourning, and healing. There is also an appendix that contains a glossary of Hebrew terms, and a brief, practical reference guide to Jewish mourning customs.

I hope and pray that this book serves as a source of strength, inspiration, and knowledge for anyone experiencing the loss of a loved one.

May you be comforted among the mourners of Zion and Jerusalem.

PART I

Chapter 1

Arrival

I didn't know what to expect when I arrived in Newark Airport on Monday, June 29th, 2009. The flight from Tel Aviv was exhausting and stressful. I was nervous. Mom had been sick for a while, but I didn't know exactly how bad her condition was.

My parents are from the old fashioned school of thought that advocates sheltering children from all bad news, even if those children are fully grown adults. I had been married for less than a year and was living in Tel Aviv with my wife Natalie. Why worry me for no good reason?

When I last saw Mom, in January of the same year, she seemed relatively fine, although she often felt tired. Over the next few months we spoke on the phone regularly. She often complained about how the medication that she was taking was making her feel run down and exhausted, but she assured me that these were just side effects which, as her doctor informed her, proved that the medication was working. I repeatedly told her that I wanted to come and see her, but she adamantly refused my offers. There was no need for me to interrupt my life and shlep all the way from Israel. In a few months she would feel better and then we would meet halfway, in Rome or Paris. She didn't want me, and especially her new daughter-in-law, to see her in her weakened state.

In May, my cousin Helene, a radiologist who was helping Mom communicate with her doctors, told me that Mom's situation was "very bad", but that she was a fighter. I was crushed by this news. I wanted to hop on the next flight to see her but, once again, she firmly told me not to come and that things would get better soon. Natalie kept telling me to go, but I felt the need to respect Mom's wishes. Perhaps the real reason was that I knew in my heart that if I went I would have to go for much longer than a week or two, and neither Natalie nor I were ready for such a lengthy, indefinite, period apart.

I wanted Mom to experience the joy of spending her final years with her only son and daughter in law, so Natalie and I decided to move to the US within a few months. When I told Mom this, I could hear the happiness break through her overwhelming weakness and fatigue. I had no idea what she was going through or how she felt, but I can just imagine the boost to her morale this news injected into her.

Over the next few weeks our conversations grew shorter and less frequent because Mom was always too tired to speak. When she mustered the strength, she would say that she knew she wouldn't live to see another year, and that she prayed to just be healthy enough to see us again. When I tried to encourage her to be strong and fight her illness, which I firmly believed she could do, she seemed to gain hope, but when she spoke to Natalie, she cried and told her to take care of me because I was all she had in the world. After one of these conversations, near the end of June, I could wait no longer. I decided to go. When I told my father, he did not protest. All he said was, "ok". That's when I knew the situation was grave.

CHAPTER 2

HISTORY

My mother, Jeane Singer, was born on May 28th, 1937 in Warsaw, Poland. Her parents, Helena and Mietzislav Rajner (Reiner) named her Janina (Yanina). Before the outbreak of World War Two, Germany and Russia signed a non aggression pact and divided Poland between them. When the Germans invaded Poland and occupied Warsaw in September 1939, my grandfather wisely decided to flee east, to the Russian occupied sector, with his wife and two year old daughter, along with thousands of other Jewish refugees. A short time later, unaware of the fate of Jews under German occupation, they boarded a train filled with Jewish refugees to return to Warsaw. Luckily, the Russians had other plans, and sent the train east to Tashkent, Uzbekistan, then part of the Soviet Union, beyond the reach of the Nazi killing machine.

Conditions in Uzbekistan were harsh. Tens of thousands of refugees died of disease and starvation. Employment was scarce. To support his wife and child, my grandfather worked in the coal mines. The backbreaking work took its toll on his health and sanity, but there was no other work. He was soon drafted into the Polish army organized by General Anders in Russia, but was subsequently rejected because he was Jewish. He was then drafted into a brigade of the Polish People's Army, named after the Polish communist Wanda Wasilewska, which fought alongside the Soviet military against the Germans.

The Polish People's Army, composed primarily of Poles deported or imprisoned by the Russian's after their occupation of eastern Poland in 1939, was not the ideal place for a Jew. To put it bluntly, it was a hot bed of anti-Semitism. Unwilling to hide his Jewish origins, grandfather was able to overcome the prejudice and anti-Semitism of his Polish comrades, rise to the rank of junior officer, and gain their, often begrudging, respect. Grandfather served in a front line communications unit. He began the war as a sergeant and ended it as a Second Lieutenant, earning the *Krzyż Walecznych* or "Medal for Merit on the Field of Glory", for valor in combat, along the way.

I remember my grandfather as a tough man with a hot temper, and I can only assume that he used these qualities to command the respect of his military comrades. Mom told me that while attending high school in post war Poland, she had an anti-Semitic male teacher who would call her "Jew" and discriminate against her in class. When grandfather found out (Mom attempted to hide the incidents from him to avoid the scene that she knew would certainly follow) he paid the teacher a visit, lifted him by the collar, and threatened to kill him if he ever dared call his daughter Jew or mistreat her in any way. Needless to say, Mom received excellent grades and never again had to deal with anti-Semitism in class. Once news of the Jewish former army officer's threat circulated, her days in school were much more pleasant.

My grandmother, Helena, was from a wealthy family that had at one time owned hat making factories in Moscow, Paris, and Warsaw. She spoke fluent French, studied piano for years in a music conservatory and played like a protégé, but it was her skill with a sewing needle that helped her survive. In Uzbekistan, grandmother earned money mending and sewing clothing and hats. With not enough time or food to adequately care for her child, she sent Mom to live in a Jewish orphanage in the area. She visited Mom as often as possible and brought her extra food and clothing. Their years in Uzbekistan, with my grandfather away, were physically and psychologically arduous. My grandfather, grandmother, and mother each nearly died as a result of illness.

When the war ended, grandfather was appointed to manage an army operated casino and entertainment center in the Polish town of Klodzko. As an officer, he was permitted to send for his family, so my grandmother and Mom, and my grandmother's sister, brother-in-law, and baby nephew boarded a military train and returned to Poland.

Poland was a dangerous place for the thousands of Jews who returned to their former homeland after the war. Nearly two thousand Jews returning to their hometowns were murdered by their former neighbors, some in organized pogroms and others in individual acts of anti-Semitic barbarity. Thousands of Jews fled Poland for the safety of the allied controlled zones of Germany, from where they proceeded to immigrate to Palestine, the United States, and other western countries. Over one hundred thousand Jews chose to remain in communist ruled Poland.

After grandfather was discharged from the army, my grandparents and mother moved to Wroclaw, a large city in south western Poland, the region where most of the Jews returning from the Soviet Union were resettled. As a result of his military service and connections, grandfather was able to secure a job as manager of a large department store and a spacious apartment in a nice part of the city.

In Wroclaw Mom had many Jewish friends, was a member of a Zionist youth group, and placed third in a national youth ski tournament. The family was able to buy kosher meat and other Jewish staples. Despite the ever present anti-Semitism, Mom and her parents, and their German shepherd Asia, lived a relatively happy and comfortable life.

In 1958, along with 50,000 other Jews, my grandparents and mother left Poland. They immigrated to Montreal, Canada, where my grandmother's sister had already moved, and settled in a predominantly Jewish area called Outremont. Grandfather didn't speak English or French, so he settled for a job in the shipping department of a large clothing factory, where he continued to work for the next twenty years. Grandmother, who spoke perfect Parisian French, designed ladies hats for a company owned by a prewar employee of her family. Mom attended McGill University, studied English, and worked as a draftsman for an architectural firm. She loved drawing and sketching, and was talented at them. Some of her originals still hang in my parents' home.

In 1961 an upstairs neighbor of hers asked if she was interested in meeting a young man, also from Poland, who lived in Toms River, New Jersey. Mom agreed. Marcus Singer, traveled to Montreal to meet her, and as they say, the rest is history. On December 24, 1961, at the Breaker's Hotel in Atlantic City, amidst a heavy snow storm, Marcus and Jeane were married by Rabbi Pesach Levovitz of Lakewood, NJ, in a lavish, black tie affair. Soon after the wedding they embarked on a honeymoon that included nearly a month in France and Italy, a month in Israel, and a return voyage on the Queen Elizabeth.

My dad, Marcus Singer, was born in Mosciska, a small town in south eastern Poland which is today part of the Ukraine, in 1933. When war broke out in September of 1939 the Russian army occupied the eastern half of Poland, including Mosciska. For the next two years the Jews living under Soviet rule enjoyed relative safety.

In 1941 Germany attacked Russia and occupied the rest of Poland and the Ukraine. The Nazis began rounding up all Jews with the help of the local population that jumped at the opportunity to rid themselves of their Jews and confiscate their property. Many Jews were murdered. The rest were herded into ghettos. Dad's family was forced into a ghetto along with the rest of the Jews in the Mosciska area.

The Singer family escaped from the ghetto and found refuge with a Polish farmer in Mosciska named Vioncek, who had worked for my grandfather before the war. They sent Dad, who was eight at the time, to live in hiding with the farmer's niece who lived in Skarżysko, a city about 350 kilometers away, in central Poland. He lived under the false identity of Roman Posazski, a young boy who had died, and did not attend school for fear of being identified as a Jew and arrested. He lived in constant fear of being discovered.

The rest of the family, including Dad's parents, older sister, three uncles, and two cousins hid in a secret room that they built in the farmer's barn for close to two years, until they were liberated by the Russian army in early 1944. My father remained in hiding for an additional eight months, until the Red Army liberated Skarżysko. He had no idea if his parents were alive until after liberation, when they sent for him.

I remember, as a child, seeing Dad wake up in the middle of the night and walk around the house in his sleep to check if anyone had broken in to search for us. He obviously still bears the scars of his terror filled childhood, which I believe prevent him from being able to display even the slightest show of weakness or vulnerability.

After the war the Singer family, realizing that the prospects for Jews in Poland were bleak, moved to Munich, in the American occupation zone of Germany, where they engaged in a variety of business ventures until finally immigrating to the United States in 1952. They settled in Toms River, NJ and bought a chicken farm. My grandfather didn't speak any English, so he figured he would be able to deal with chickens who, he joked, understood Yiddish.

After returning from their honeymoon, my parents moved to a luxurious river view apartment in Riverdale, NY. Mom often reminisced about those spectacular views. A couple of years later they moved to a modest apartment in Elizabeth, NJ where I was born on March 3, 1966. After almost a decade in Elizabeth, we moved to the small town of Mountainside, about a half hour to the west, where Mom lived until her passing. She loved the hills and abundance of trees in Mountainside, and never missed an opportunity to praise her new hometown.

CHAPTER 3

BREAST CANCER

About seven years prior to her passing, Mom was diagnosed with breast cancer. As far as I know, she suffered serious health problems only twice before. The first time was as a toddler in Uzbekistan, when she contracted Typhus while in the orphanage. The second was when giving birth to me. Mom's doctors neglected to completely remove her placenta, causing infection and bleeding. She fully recovered physically, but the experience left psychological scars which, as she always admitted, prevented her from having more children.

Mom occasionally wished that she had had a girl whom she could take shopping and outfit in the latest fashion. Her wish finally came true when she took my wife shopping on several occasions and bought her the most fashionable handbags and shoes, stunning jewelry, and whatever else she felt my wife needed.

Money was no object to Mom. All that mattered was for her daughter-in-law to have the best of everything. Her greatest joy was introducing my wife to anyone she spoke to, including the salespeople. "This is my daughter-in-law," she would proudly beam. Although she only had a few opportunities to spend time alone with her daughter-in-law, the love and kindness Mom showered upon Natalie left a lasting impression on her.

When Mom first told me that she had breast cancer, I was on the other end of a phone line in my Manhattan apartment. She tried to reassure me that everything would be alright, but a huge dam inside of me burst unleashing a flood of tears more powerful than anything I remember experiencing since childhood. I don't recall whether I was still on the phone when I cried or whether I was able to hold back my tears and mumble a few words before hanging up. It doesn't really matter. Either way, she knew I was crying. Mothers can sense when their children are devastated.

I never knew how much Mom suffered during her battle with cancer, primarily because she didn't tell me. She didn't want me to worry. What good would that do? She stood tough throughout the entire ordeal, which included a partial Mastectomy and Chemotherapy. While she occasionally would open up and tell me how tired or scared she was, she refused to let anyone besides family know that she was sick. Mom continued running her business as if nothing was wrong. When her hair began to fall out as a result of the Chemotherapy, she donned a wig that looked almost identical to her real hair so that no one would know. She told me not to reveal to anyone that she wore a wig, not even to my wife. In the nearly seven years she wore that wig, only a handful people ever figured it out. Part of me is even reluctant to reveal her secret in these pages, but I believe that describing her tremendous strength of character and fighting spirit honors her memory.

Many cancer patients deal with their illness by fully and openly accepting it, and refuse to wear wigs to hide the effects of their treatment. Mom refused to accept her illness and allow it to rule over her. When the cancer took her hair, she wore a wig. When it drained her energy, she pushed herself harder. She would not show any weakness. She never stopped fighting. She inherited the stubborn determination and toughness of her father, the officer, and would never surrender.

She won. The course of treatment she received, combined with her fierce will to survive, forced the cancer into remission, where it would remain for the next six years.

CHAPTER 4

NATALIE

In October of 2007 I went to Israel for a few months of spiritual and emotional rejuvenation, and met Natalie. Born in London, Natalie chose to move to Israel after graduating from high school, and has never regretted her decision. Her parents and most of her five married siblings have followed her lead. We dated for just over six months before I returned to NY to "think". A week later I asked her to join me, and we got engaged. Before I popped the question I took her home to meet my parents.

I had spoken to Mom about Natalie many times, and she had encouraged me to get engaged. It might seem as though she would have wanted me to marry just about anyone at this point (I was 42), but that wasn't the case. Mom was always sensitive to my personal needs and wanted me to be truly happy. From what I've heard, she was even willing to accept that I might be gay (not that there's anything wrong with that), if that's who I was. As she often reminded me, "You will always be my son, and I will always love you."

Just to clarify, the reason why Mom thought I might be gay is because I never spoke to her about the girls I was dating. I didn't want to get her hopes up. I learned my lesson from the time I brought a girl home whom I had been dating for a few months. It wasn't a planned, formal meeting, just a random visit to the house on our way to another destination. She and Mom were in the same room for only a few moments and exchanged just a few words of greetings but, for the next decade, Mom would always ask, "I don't understand, what was wrong with her?"

I cannot even imagine the anticipation my parents, especially Mom, felt as they waited for me to arrive with their potential daughter-in-law. I'm sure Mom and Natalie were both nervous. I'm pretty sure my Dad wasn't. He rarely is. I wasn't nervous in the least. I was positive that my parents would love Natalie. I was right (as usual!). They fell in love with her that first night. The next day, Friday, we got engaged and on Sunday we returned to my parents' home to formally celebrate.

Mom prepared a gourmet dinner for us. She loved to cook, and was great at it. She took pride in her culinary creations, and derived immense satisfaction from the approbation showered upon her by her satisfied guests. Her greatest joy came from watching my father and me enjoy the food she lovingly made for us. She would sit at the table and watch me eat to see my reaction. She was rarely disappointed.

One of her most sought after dishes was one that I don't remember her making since I was a child. It had a Polish name that translates into "calf's foot in gelatin (*galareta*, in Polish)" and looked like clear jello filled with meat. My parents would occasionally host house parties at which, among other old world delicacies, Mom would serve huge trays of the jello stuff, which would quickly disappear onto the plates and into the mouths of her Polish born friends. I think you have to have been born in Poland to like the stuff. I never touched it. The Polish gang, on the other hand, devoured every last morsel of it. Mom was known as the best cook in the group, perhaps solely due to those calf's feet in gelatin.

CHAPTER 5

MOVING

Natalie returned to Israel a week later to begin planning our wedding, while I began packing my belongings and saying my goodbyes. On July 10th, 2008 I moved to Israel and became a citizen of the Jewish state.

I imagine that it was difficult for Mom to see me go, but I know she was happy that I had found happiness and was getting married. She took my moving thousands of miles away in stride. "A man moves to where his wife wants to be and where her family is," she said. "It's part of life, the way things go, and I'll have to deal with it."

This ability to take life in stride and deal with whatever happens is a quality prevalent among Holocaust survivors that has been transplanted into the Israeli psyche. "Ein Breirah" is Hebrew for "there is no other choice". This is what we have, so this is what we must deal with. What other reaction can one who has experienced incredible hardship and survived have?

When Jews emerged from concentration camps and hiding places, after surviving mass murder, brutalization, starvation, disease, and the constant terror of the hunted, they were physically and mentally broken. Their lives were destroyed, their families and loved ones murdered, their world turned upside down. They could have easily given up, but they didn't. They continued living, loving, working, laughing. They married, had children, built homes, schools, businesses, and a country of their own with an army that would never again permit their destruction.

Mom was a survivor. She played the hand dealt her, good or bad, and made the best of her situation. She would have done well in Israel. I guess I consider myself a survivor too.

CHAPTER 6

CELEBRATIONS

It was around this time that the doctors discovered cancer cells in Mom's lymph nodes, the malignancy of which they would determine upon her return from Israel. Not even the prospect of going through another bout with the deadly illness could stop her from enjoying her son's wedding to the fullest. As soon as she stepped off the plane into the Tel Aviv sunshine, she was re-energized. Over the next few days she and Dad went out to dinner with Natalie's parents, hosted a dinner at the Tel Aviv Hilton for Natalie's siblings, and went on a drive through the Galilee to the Kinneret with Natalie and I. It was as if she had never been sick.

One of the highlights of the trip for Mom was seeing her best friend, Rachela Laor. Mom had been friends with Rachela in Poland, where they were members of the same Zionist youth group. Rachela immigrated to Israel with her parents around the same time Mom immigrated to Canada. They continued a long distance friendship that lasted over fifty years. Mom was thrilled to have Rachela sit with her at my wedding. Unfortunately, Rachela lost her own battle with cancer a few months after Mom's passing.

Mom had a special place in her heart for Israel. As a teenager, she had often contemplated joining her many friends who moved there from Poland. She loved listening to Israeli music. Although she never learned Hebrew, she enjoyed singing the few Israeli folksongs she had learned in her youth group days.

The climax of her Israel trip, and probably her life, was my wedding. It might have been a bit difficult for her to simply be a guest at her son's wedding, instead of the wedding planner and hostess, but she certainly didn't display anything but happiness and praise. This was primarily because Natalie, and Natalie's mother, happen to have the same refined, discerning taste and elegance as she had, so everything she saw at the wedding received her unequivocal approval.

Some of my closest relatives made the journey from New Jersey to Jerusalem for the wedding, and Mom made sure that they were comfortable and taken care of. She hosted a *Shabbat* dinner and lunch for the family at the David Citadel Hotel, where we stayed and where the wedding was held. It meant a lot to her to have our side of the family present. The wedding was beautiful, and Mom enjoyed every moment of it. The wedding photos of her speak for themselves.

Natalie and I visited my parents in mid September for a few weeks and again around the Christmas and New Year's holiday break. That New Year's Eve was especially significant for Mom.

Mom always loved to go out on the town. For most of my childhood and adult years, my parents would drive to Manhattan every Saturday night and enjoy dinner and dancing at one of a few night clubs that they loved. My parents loved dancing, and were expert at it. They actually knew the steps to all of the classic ballroom dances, not just the improvised moves of novices trying to impress. No, they were the real thing on the dance floor, and drew admiring glances from everyone watching.

Two nights that were particularly important for Mom to celebrate on were December 24th, her wedding anniversary, and New Year's Eve. She always wished for the day when I, and a special female companion, would join her and Dad. That moment was finally within reach when Natalie and I came to visit. I'm sure Mom thought about New Year's Eve a lot in the weeks before we arrived. She planned the evening in detail and even invited a few of her close friends from the Calf's Foot eating crowd to join us. She beamed throughout the entire night. I think it was one of her happiest nights out ever. I'm grateful that I could give her that.

Our ten day visit was wonderful for all of us. We said goodbye confident that, despite Mom's upcoming cancer treatment, we would enjoy more good times together in the very near future.

CHAPTER 7

LIVER

I followed Mom's condition, over the next few months, based on the information she gave me during our regular phone conversations. I don't think I ever got the complete description of her condition, either because she wanted to avoid worrying me or because she didn't fully understand it herself. The answer probably lies somewhere between the two. The little I did know was that the doctors began treating the cancer in her lymph nodes with chemotherapy, but stopped the treatment after the first dose, when they discovered that her liver was damaged.

Mom had a chronic case of Hepatitis-B virus for most of her life. It's unclear how or when she was infected, but I suspect that it was either passed on from my grandmother (who I remember suffering from it right before her death) or contracted amidst the abysmal conditions during her time in Uzbekistan. Chronic Hepatitis doesn't manifest any symptoms, but it slowly damages the liver. The chemotherapy she received for her lymph node cancer probably damaged her immune system, which caused an acute inflammation of the Hepatitis-B virus. The virus then aggressively attacked the liver, slowly causing it to fail. Mom began to retain water which caused pronounced swelling in her arms, legs, and face. She also became fatigued. She was given medication to counter the virus, and a diuretic to relieve the swelling. In place of the chemo, she began receiving radiation treatment to fight her cancer.

When I spoke to her on the phone she was often too tired to converse for more than a few moments. She reiterated that her fatigue was a side effect of her liver medication, and that her doctor told her that it was a sign that the medication was working. It's unclear to me whether this was the doctor's way of giving Mom hope, or whether he actually believed it to be true. In any case, it gave Mom strength to fight her illness.

Up until her last days Mom and Dad were unaware of actually how terminal her condition was. In fact, just two weeks before her death, her liver doctor gave her a new and stronger liver drug and told her to return to see him in six months. This doctor is considered to be the top in his specialty, and yet, he told her to come back in six months. I can't imagine that he didn't know the severity of her condition and how quickly her liver could fail. When he spoke to us a little over a week later in the intensive care waiting room of St. Barnabas hospital in Livingston NJ, he seemed confident enough to tell me and Dad that Mom probably wouldn't survive the day. Why, then, did he tell Mom to see him in six months? Was he simply giving her false hope?

I firmly believe that prayer, hope, and raw determination play a major role in combating illness. The will to live is what, in many cases, kept concentration camp inmates alive while those who lost their will to survive perished. I also believe in the right to know the truth about your condition so that you can make informed decisions regarding how to proceed. Patients need time to prepare for death, to spend time with loved ones, to complete unfinished business, and to say their goodbyes. False hope deprives them, and their loved ones, of those important opportunities and precious moments. Had we known the truth earlier, I could have spent another precious week with Mom, with her fully conscious, in her own home. Doctors must be sensitive and optimistic, but they must also be honest when they give their patients their diagnosis.

By mid June Mom's condition was deteriorating rapidly. Her arms and legs were swollen to abnormal proportions. Her skin was turning yellow. She was too weak to walk and could barely. Her liver was failing. I knew I had to see her.

Chapter 8

Emergency

I came home from the airport on June 29th and found Mom lying on the coach, unable to move. She was too swollen and weak to walk without assistance. Although she could barely speak, she managed to tell me that she was happy I was with her. I tried to comfort her, telling her that everything would be ok, but I was shocked and terrified by her condition.

The next morning, Tuesday June 30th, Dad and I took Mom to St. Barnabas Hospital for her scheduled radiation treatment. That she continued to receive these treatments despite her condition is a testament to the total lack of coordination and communication between her three doctors, all well known and respected specialists. There was the liver doctor, the radiation doctor, and the cancer doctor, and each one focused on his particular task without taking the time to communicate with his colleagues. In fact, the radiation doctor was so shocked to see the condition Mom was in as a result of her liver disease that he personally called her liver doctor to inform him. I was going to say "to reprimand him", which is what he should have done, but from my experience with specialist physicians, I hardly think the conversation took on a tone of reprimand. Renowned specialists don't reprimand each other over ordinary patients. Perhaps he only left him a message.

During Mom's entire period of illness my cousin Helene and my cousin Steven, a well connected cardiologist, made phone calls to Mom's doctors to get a first hand understanding of her condition. Sometimes the information that doctors give their patients gets misunderstood. It often takes another doctor to fully understand a diagnosis, and to be able to intelligently question it if necessary. Also, while doctors are often too busy to promptly answer patient calls, they seem to free up when there is an MD on the other end of the line. Professional courtesy, I guess. Having an interested family member in the medical profession can make a patient's life much easier, but it's no guarantee.

After administering her radiation treatment that Tuesday morning, the doctor sat me and Dad down and told us that Mom's condition was terminal and that she probably wouldn't live for more than a few more days, perhaps a week. We were in shock. This was news none of her doctors had told us before. I called Helene and she was shocked too. We tried to get in touch with the liver specialist, but he was unreachable. There was no one in charge to tell us what to do.

Steven prevailed upon Mom's oncologist, an old colleague of his, to coordinate her treatment. We immediately went to his office in the main hospital building for an examination. His nurse took Mom's blood pressure, was startled at how low it was, and immediately rushed her to the emergency room. She was in critical condition.

The liver filters waste products and toxins, including sodium, from the blood stream. Liver damage frequently affects the kidneys, preventing them from properly eliminating excess sodium from the body, causing fluid retention and swelling. Mom was taking diuretics to drain the excess fluid, but these were also depleting her sodium level. When she was taken to the emergency room her sodium levels were life threateningly low, causing her to fall into a coma. The doctors infused her with sodium to raise her level, while at the same time continuing the diuretics to expel the fluids, something her body could no longer accomplish independently. This delicate balancing act went on for most of the day.

I called Helene, who promptly arrived and recognized the chief emergency room resident as a former colleague of hers. I'm sure that the ER staff provides the same level of care and attention to all of their patients, but I think that extra connection with a fellow physician whose aunt's life was in their hands made a positive difference. They succeeded in stabilizing Mom and, late that night, moved her to the intensive care ward.

CHAPTER 9

CONSENT

At about 4:30am the next morning, Wednesday July 1st, I heard Dad's cell phone ring. He had left it downstairs when he came home from the hospital a few hours earlier, after waiting for Mom to be transferred to the intensive care unit. Had the door to my bedroom been closed, as it usually is when I sleep, I wouldn't have heard the soft ring of the phone, but I had left the door open and just happened to have awoken moments before the call. Perhaps it was due to my jet lag from the Israel flight, but I think it was the deep, spiritual connection between mother and son that alerted me. It prevented me from sleeping soundly while Mom suffered, fighting for her life. It tore at my soul.

I ran downstairs and answered the phone with trepidation. A 4:30am phone call is never good news. It was the intensive care hospitalist. She said that Mom was bleeding internally in her stomach, and she needed our consent to perform a procedure to stop it. The timing of the call combined with the difficulty I had in understanding the doctor's accent, and the phrase "require your consent", drove me into a frenzy. I handed Dad the phone and he gave consent. Then I cried uncontrollably. I thought that this was it, the end. Why else would they call at 4:30am and ask for our consent? I told Dad we had to rush to the hospital immediately to be with Mom in her final moments. We couldn't let her die alone.

I called Natalie, hysterical, and told her she had to come as soon as possible. She was on the Golan Heights, on a work assignment for the British Embassy, when I called. Several hours later she was on a Continental flight to Newark.

Dad and I were in the intensive care unit waiting area by 5:50am. We were told that Mom had stabilized, but was still in critical condition. At approximately 9:00am the liver specialist, previously unreachable, entered the waiting room. He sat next to us and, in what was probably his most sensitive tone, bluntly told us that Mom had no chance of surviving more than a day or two. Sorry. Done. He left. Our lives were shattered. I saw my father cry for the first time. I, once again, wept uncontrollably.

The Talmud teaches that one should not give up hoping for a miracle even when the sword is against one's throat. Paradoxically, the Talmud also teaches that one should avoid dangerous, life threatening, situations because one should not rely on a miracle to save him. What, then, is the Talmud's advice regarding miracles? As usual, both Talmudic statements are correct. One should not enter into a situation relying upon miraculous salvation, but once in the situation, one should never give up hoping for a miracle. The belief in sudden, miraculous salvation is a fundamental principle of Judaism. Since God is omnipotent, nothing is out of the question.

The doctor had pronounced his medical judgement, but God had not pronounced His. Mom was still alive, and I would not give up hope. We needed a miracle.

CHAPTER 10

PRAYER

The only thing I could do while Mom lay unconscious in intensive care, fighting for her life, was pray. I am an Orthodox Rabbi. I tell you this not to claim any spiritual advantage or special access to a designated hotline to God. The title of Orthodox Rabbi carries with it no spiritual privileges beyond those possessed by any other human being. The only thing it does is certify that the ideas and explanations I present to you regarding Jewish spirituality, ritual, and philosophy are firmly rooted in, and based upon, an authentic and unbroken tradition stretching back thousands of years.

Jewish prayer is called "service of the heart" throughout rabbinic literature. It is an expression of Man's deepest emotions and yearnings, and a vehicle of praise, supplication, comfort, or thanksgiving. Prayer is commonly expressed through the spoken word, but it is in no way confined to that medium. Sometimes words are simply not sufficient to convey intense emotions. Sometimes an emotional experience is so intense that one is unable to utter a coherent phrase. In those instances, music can serve as the expressive medium of prayer.

A simple melody can potentially express more raw emotion than the most complex poetry. The prime example of this in Jewish tradition is the sounding of the *Shofar*, the ram's horn, on *Rosh Hashanah*, the Jewish day of judgement. The sounds of the *Shofar* represent our cries of repentance at a time when we know that we are unworthy and unable to formulate the proper words to plead with on our behalf. That simple, basic sound emanating from a modest, unadorned ram's horn expresses innate contrition and pleading in a way that we could never fully express in words.

There's a form of prayer even more powerful than the purest *Shofar* blast or the most enchanting supplicative melody: crying. The different sounds of the *Shofar*, long, medium, and staccato, are meant to mimic different types of cries. Crying exposes our greatest fears and pain, leaving us defenseless and vulnerable. When we cry to God we surrender ourselves and our fate to Him, and place ourselves completely at the grace of His mercy. We have nothing to offer in exchange for that mercy. We approach Him as a child approaches a parent, offering only our contrition, and hope that God treats us like a loving parent who cannot bear to see his children suffer helplessly. Crying not only takes the place of verbal prayer. It transforms the person crying into a prayer. This is best expressed by the Psalmist King David who wrote, "I am a prayer".

Can you imagine actually being a prayer? Picture a beggar with his hand outstretched. He doesn't have to verbally ask you for money. His entire being screams his request. Just one look at him is all you need to know exactly what he needs. During Mom's last days, I became a prayer. Everything I did, every gesture, every tear, was a prayer for God to help her.

I'm not a big crier. Since my Dad never cried, I presumed that men don't cry. When they feel like crying, they fight back the tears and express their emotions with somber or stern facial expressions and heavy sighs. When I get the overwhelming urge to burst into tears at a wedding ceremony or sappy movie, I apply every ounce of strength I can muster to hold back my tears, to prevent anyone from witnessing my weakness. When I'm alone I let the tears flow, because if no one sees it, it's like it never happened. My manhood remains intact and unaffected. During Mom's illness I felt like crying all the time, but I did so only in front of my wife and my father, and only when I could no longer hold back.

Only twice during Mom's hospitalization was I unable to hold back my tears. The first time was on that morning when Mom's liver specialist informed us to begin preparing for the inevitable. I didn't care that there was a woman sitting in the waiting room, watching me. I did what I needed to do.

The second time was after Mom was moved from the intensive care ward to a hospital room. Natalie and I took a break from staying by Mom's bedside and went outside to a wooded area with a beautiful pond, next to the hospital parking lot. It was a pristine day, sunny, cool, everything was perfect. I sat on a rock next to the pond and took in the natural beauty surrounding me, but I couldn't appreciate any of it. The tension, the sadness, the feeling of helplessness were too much for me to bear. All I could see was darkness and pain. I broke down and cried. Once the walls that had held back days, perhaps weeks, of tears crumbled, my tears gushed forth, unstoppable, leaving me with room for new tears.

It was when I prayed alone that my tears flowed most powerfully. I was like a small child weeping before his father, begging, pleading, beseeching, seeking comfort, assistance, acknowledgement. I believe that I was heard, although the answer I received was not what I had hoped for. I felt comforted knowing that I was not alone in my pain and sorrow. My Father in Heaven was there with me. I was reassured that what was meant to be would ultimately be for the best, part of a grand divine plan that my mortal mind could not comprehend. Perhaps it would become clear at some point in the future, after a few years or a few centuries. Regardless of the outcome, I never stopped being a prayer, not even for a moment.

CHAPTER 11

WORDS

My extolling of non verbal prayer does not, in the least, diminish my love of, and reliance upon, the verbal form. Traditionally, prayer has been expressed through words, emanating from the depths of the soul. In Psalm 120, King David cries,

> *From the depths I call out to You, God. My God, hear my voice, let Your ears be attentive to the voice of my supplication.*

Prayers can be recited in any language that the supplicant understands. In Jewish tradition, the designated and preferred language of prayer is Hebrew. According to the bible, God created the world with a series of utterances. God said, "let there be light", "let there be luminaries in the heavens", "let there be fish in the sea and birds in the sky", and so on, until creation was completed. According to Jewish mystical tradition, the language God used to create with was Hebrew.

The twenty six letters of the Hebrew alphabet are thus the building blocks of creation, and contain within them the energy to create. As a result, the Hebrew language is imbued with spiritual powers that simply don't exist in any other language.

The ancient Jewish sages and mystics recognized this power, and combined the letters into words and sentences to harness and release the unique energy force within the specific letters used. These letter and word combinations form spiritual codes that can affect, or even manipulate, the spiritual forces through which God interacts with the world. Each prayer composed by the sages affects a particular spiritual force. For example, the letters and words that make up the traditional Jewish healing supplications form mystical combinations that can counter the spiritual forces of illness and unlock the spiritual portals of healing.

Hebrew has been the Jewish prayer language for thousands of years. The Patriarchs, Abraham, Isaac, and Jacob, and the Matriarchs, Sarah, Rebecca, Rachel, and Leah prayed in Hebrew. The great Jewish prophets including Moses, Aaron, Joshua, Samuel, Deborah, Nathan, Elijah, Jonah, Isaiah, Jeremiah, Ezekiel, did the same. Rabbis, mystics, holy men, and simple, ordinary men, women, and children have beseeched God in Hebrew throughout Jewish history, from the slave pits of Egypt, to the inquisitions and expulsions of Medieval Europe, to the death camps of Nazi Germany. When we pray in Hebrew we forge a direct connection with our ancestors and our heritage. Our prayers combine with theirs to form a powerful force of supplication.

Reliance on the merit of righteous ancestors plays a central role in Jewish prayer. The liturgy frequently highlights the relationship of the supplicant to the Patriarchs Abraham, Isaac, and Jacob. They are viewed not as distant holy figures of the past, but rather as actual grandparents prepared to assist and protect their grandchildren. When we pray, we remind God of the loyalty and righteousness of these grandparents and beseech him to heed our prayers, not because we deserve to be heard, but because they did. We ask God to, "do it for their sake, if not for ours."

Our reliance on the merit of our ancestors is not confined to the Patriarchs. Any person who we feel merits divine attention, who we identify with, and with whom we can claim a familial or spiritual relationship can help our prayers succeed. A prominent mystic rabbi was once approached by a religious man who told him that he could not concentrate on his prayers, and asked him for advice on how to attain the proper level of concentration during prayer. The rabbi advised him to imagine a great religious personality whom he connected with, and to attach his own prayers to the prayers of that individual. In that way his prayers would reach the heavens together with the prayers of that individual.

I called upon all of my holy ancestors to help carry my prayers and intercede on Mom's behalf. I sent my Mom's Hebrew name (Yehudit) and the name of her mother (Chaya Rochel) to all of my friends and acquaintances and asked them to pray for her. Hundreds of people, in America and Israel, did.

There's something special and powerful that occurs when an entire community of people joins together in prayer for a common purpose. Disparate individuals are transformed into a single, united, entity whose power is greater than the sum total of its individual parts. This new entity, or community, can petition God with confidence, even a bit of "chutzpah", relying on

God's mercy towards His children when they come before Him in unity and brotherhood.

A Hasidic parable tells of a rare, exquisite bird that was perched on top of a tall tree. Many of the townspeople tried to capture the bird, but none were able to reach it. Then they joined together and stood on each other's shoulders, forming a ladder that reached to the top of the tree, and caught the bird. Had just one of the townspeople not joined in the endeavor, the ladder would not have reached high enough. Only when they all worked together as one could they capture their treasure.

This explains the power of communal prayer, and why it plays such an important role in Jewish ritual. Certain prayers can only be recited in the company of ten adult Jewish males, the minimum number required to be considered a community. The most famous of these prayers is the *Kaddish,* the mourner's prayer, which I'll discuss in depth in a later chapter of this book. It's important to find a community or prayer group whose members you feel connected to, and where you feel comfortable speaking to God.

CHAPTER 12

REBBE

When I initially called Natalie upon seeing Mom immobilized on the sofa, Natalie promised to visit a Chassidic Rabbi who lived around the corner from our Tel Aviv home, to ask for his blessing and prayers. Rabbi Avraham Shimshon Halpern is known as the Vasloy *Rebbe*. Vasloy is the town in Romania where his grandfather served as Chassidic Rebbe in the early part of the twentieth century. The Vasloy Rebbe has a small synagogue (*shteible*, in Yiddish) on Ben Gurion Street, just a few blocks from the Tel Aviv beach, where he serves Jews of all levels of religious observance, and where I used to pray every Friday night.

The Friday night prayer service is called "*Kabbalat Shabbat* - Welcoming the Sabbath" and is highlighted by several prayers that are traditionally sung by the congregation. The *Rebbe*, wearing traditional Chassidic garb and a long white beard, usually led the small but full congregation as cantor. He would always sing the primary prayer, "*Lecha Dodi*", in a haunting melody that I had never heard before. It took me many weeks to learn the melody but once I did, it became my favorite. The melody, a waltz, has three sections, each one an emotional supplication, building in intensity until the final section, which pleadingly cries out for salvation. Sung resoundingly by the entire congregation, that third section always brought me to the brink of tears. It connected me to generations of righteous men and women who cried out to God using that very same melody. I sang this melody many times during Mom's illness, and it always gave me strength and comfort. I rarely got through it without weeping.

Natalie rang the doorbell to the Rebbe's *shteible* and was surprised when the Rebbe himself opened the door. She burst into tears. He took her into his office and she explained why she was there. He prayed for Mom's recovery and gave Natalie a small coin, blessed by his saintly father, for Mom to keep with her. Did the coin possess magical healing powers? Probably not intrinsic power, but it did carry within it the power of hope. I also feel that it's significant to hold something that was once handled and blessed by a holy man. Perhaps some of his positive spiritual energy rubbed off onto it. I couldn't give Mom the coin because she had nowhere to keep it in her hospital gown, but I told her about it and kept it in my wallet. I would act as her proxy. I still carry that coin in my wallet.

Natalie and I were comforted to know that a holy man was praying for Mom. The Rebbe wasn't the only great rabbi praying for her. Our landlord in Tel Aviv passed along Mom's name to his mother, who happened to be in contact with the chief rabbi of the State of Israel. She passed him the name, and he said a special prayer on Mom's behalf.

Are the prayers of rabbis and holy men more effective than those of ordinary people? Ignoring all the stories and legends of how the prayers of holy people were miraculously answered, I simply think that the more spiritually aware and connected a person is, the greater the chance that his prayers will have an impact in the spiritual realm. You don't have to be a rabbi or holy man to lead a spiritually intense life, but it's nice to know that there are people out there who are dedicated to spirituality and who can help you connect with it.

CHAPTER 13

DIVINE DECREE

There are two explanations in Jewish philosophical thought regarding how prayer can affect the supplicant. One theory postulates that prayer can actually change the supplicant's destiny by causing his decreed fate to be remanded. Every occurrence in the physical world is caused by a divine decree, or judgment, in the spiritual world. Prayer is a tool that can change that divine decree. By undoing the underlying spiritual decree, the supplicant can neutralize its worldly effect. This is a major theme in the Jewish High Holiday liturgy, where it explicitly states, "repentance, prayer, and charity avert the evil of the decree."

According to this theory, people other than the subject of the divine decree can attempt to have the decree rescinded. Other people may even have a better chance of success, if they are more deserving of divine intervention than the subject. When an entire community joins together, the chances of success are greater.

Conceptualizing "divine decree" is difficult. It exists solely in the spiritual realm but has the power to activate forces in the physical world. For example, a divine decree for someone to get sick will activate the negative forces in and around the body, which had previously been dormant. These negative forces are what cause the illness. How exactly this happens is a mystery far beyond the scope of this book.

I am not a scientist. I never took a physics course and I have almost no knowledge of mathematics above the level of simple algebra. My information regarding forces and energy comes primarily from New Age theories that apply the principles of quantum physics to attempt to quantify the forces activated by the divine decree, in order to affect them. Now that I've given you my disclaimer, let me try to explain my non-scientific understanding of how this works.

Everything is made up of molecules. Altering the structure of these molecules changes the physical properties of the matter that they are components of. Dr. Masaru Emoto, a Japanese Doctor of Alternative Medicine, performed a series of experiments on water to prove that thoughts and feelings can affect molecular structure. He developed a technique to photograph newly formed crystals of frozen water samples using a powerful microscope along with high-speed photography. Dr. Emoto discovered that crystals formed in frozen water reveal changes when specific, concentrated thoughts are directed toward them. He found that water from clear springs and water that was exposed to loving words and messages or a blessing by a Buddhist monk showed brilliant, complex, and colorful snowflake patterns. In contrast, polluted water or water exposed to negative thoughts and messages formed incomplete, asymmetrical patterns with dull colors.

If we accept the veracity of his results, Emoto's conclusions are revolutionary. Half the world is water. Our body is three quarters water. If we can affect the structure of water with our thoughts and words, we can affect our bodies and the world around us. Extending this theory beyond water, anything composed of molecules can be affected. According to theories of quantum mechanics, distance does not create a barrier between objects. Therefore, we can affect things regardless of our distance from them.

The concept of affecting the molecular structure of matter through words and thoughts is found in the teachings of the Kabbalists and Hasidic masters, in the context of prayer and blessings.

Prayer is a tool we use to transform ourselves and the world around us. When we pray for someone's healing, including our own, we attempt to influence the molecular structure of the body to fight the illness plaguing it. We are literally trying to reverse, or at least modify, the negative effects of the divine decree. The more spiritually sensitive and developed the supplicant, the greater effect his prayers can have. This is why we ask those we consider holy to pray for us.

Jewish ritual instructs us to recite a blessing before eating or drinking. The content of the blessing is specific to the category of the food or drink. The blessing we recite affects the molecular structure of the food imbuing it with, what we'll call, positive energy. That positive energy then becomes part of our body, and serves to uplift us spiritually and physically. This gives real meaning to the phrase, "you are what you eat." This can also give greater meaning to the Jewish kosher laws, which permit and prohibit specific foods for consumption. The molecular structure of a non-kosher foodstuff adversely affects the molecular structure of a healthy Jewish body while having no negative effect on a non-Jew. I specify "healthy" because according to Jewish law, a sick person who must eat is permitted to eat non-kosher food if kosher food is unavailable. The sick person's molecular structure is not adversely affected by the non-kosher food.

The morning prayer service, by far the longest and most intricate of the three daily Jewish prayer services, can literally transform the supplicant into a positive, healthy, and productive person. It's no coincidence that the Hebrew term for prayer is constructed in the reflexive grammatical form. When we pray, we literally change ourselves.

I prayed so hard to reverse Mom's negative divine decree. I prayed for the cancer cells and the hepatitis virus to disappear, and for her liver to rejuvenate and function normally. It didn't matter that, for most of the time, I was thousands of miles away in Israel. We were connected by the most powerful bond, the bond between mother and child, which could not be interrupted by time or distance.

I meditated every night before bed. I visualized the evil cancer cells, on fire with rage, viciously attacking Mom's body. Then I visualized dousing them with water, extinguishing their flames, and flushing them away.

I believe that the cancer alone could have been defeated, but the hepatitis virus was unstoppable. Had I known about the virus prior to the few weeks before Mom's death, perhaps I could have helped fight it. Perhaps the targeted prayers and tears of an only child would have been strong enough to defeat the divine decree that attacked in the form of a microscopic virus? I'll never know for certain. What is certain is that sometimes a negative divine decree is part of a person's destiny, and nothing, no matter how powerful the prayer or how poignant the tears, can change it.

CHAPTER 14

NEW IDENTITY

Another theory explaining how prayer affects the supplicant is that it transforms him into a new person, with a new identity, who is not the target of the divine decree. Praying motivates a person to reflect on his life, improve his relationships, and modify his behavior for the better. Judaism calls this repentance. Regardless of what a person has done in the past, when he sincerely repents he is considered a new person with a clean slate. The judgments and decrees attached to the old person, the sinner, are no longer applicable, for the sinner no longer exists. For example, there is a Jewish custom to change the name of a terminally ill person, usually by adding a name meaning life (i.e. Chaim, Chaya). This new identity is meant to provide the person with a new, and hopefully healthier, destiny.

The performance of *Mitzvot* and good deeds also transforms a person and can cause an evil decree to be rescinded. For example, Mr. Davis, stricken by illness, has 100 merits. If Mr. Davis increases his merits to 150, he is no longer the same Mr. Davis-100 who has a decree of illness against him. He is now Mr. Davis-150, with no decrees in his file.

The challenge is that we have absolutely no idea what the divine set of accounting rules are and how merits are valued. The factors that may be taken into account by the divine judgment are impossible for human beings to account for or even comprehend. The best we can do is to try to increase our merits and hope for the best.

A fundamental concept in Jewish philosophy is that all Jews are metaphysically connected. This concept can be applied to all human beings. Based on this, I can perform a merit for someone else. In addition to receiving credit for my merit, the beneficiary also gains a merit for causing me to act meritoriously. The more people praying and performing good deeds on someone's behalf, the greater the merit that accumulates for that person. I'm certain that the hundreds, perhaps thousands, of individuals who prayed for Mom and performed good deeds in her merit were an integral part of her battle against her illness.

There is one more way of affecting the fate of another. A person can attach himself to another, tying together their fates and destinies. It's almost like saying, "if you want to fight him, you'll have to fight me." In the bible, Judah ties his fate to his younger brother Benjamin in order to guarantee his safety. I tied my fate to Mom's, threw all of my merits into her account ledger, and begged God to view us as one new entity deserving of divine mercy. I became her guarantor. My guarantee was not accepted.

Chapter 15

Hope

On Wednesday morning, July 1st, Dad and I sat in the intensive care waiting room, our hopes shattered by a liver specialist, waiting for the opportunity to see Mom. After a few hours of suffering through the pain and anxiety of not knowing her condition, we were allowed into the unit to see her. She was unconscious and attached to oxygen and tubes that infused her with the fluids she needed and drained the fluids she didn't. Her condition was critical. The doctors didn't know if she would regain consciousness.

I barely moved from Mom's side. I prayed. I begged her to wake up. She did. She spoke. She was aware of everything. I rejoiced. I regained hope. It didn't matter that her prognosis was terminal and that the doctors gave her no hope of living more than a day or two. I had another moment with Mom. Perhaps I would get another, then another. Every moment with her was precious. Every moment of life is precious.

Mom was conscious for just minutes at a time. It was as if she was so exhausted that she couldn't keep her eyes open. Unfortunately, exhaustion was only part of it. She was falling in and out of the hepatic coma caused by her liver failure. The doctors continued the same delicate fluid balancing act that they had performed in the emergency room, not knowing if they would succeed in stabilizing her.

The chief resident explained Mom's condition to us and said that there was a fair chance that she would be stabilized. He confirmed that her liver was failing and that her chances of survival were grim, but he did so with a sensitivity that gave us the tiniest glimmer of hope. To be clear, he didn't give us false hope or mislead us with even minimal optimism. He simply didn't smash any belief we might have in a miraculous recovery. I don't know if he was a religious man or not, but he obviously believed in a God that he acknowledged was not him. Only God has the power of life and death.

When we left late that night we were reassured that Mom would, in all probability, make it through the night. I wouldn't have left had I thought otherwise.

CHAPTER 16

REUNION

My sleep that night was light and restless, filled with bad dreams. Every night was like that for me now. My mind was preoccupied with Mom. Natalie was scheduled to land at Newark at around 5:00am, so I didn't have much time to sleep in any case.

Throughout the night I could hear Rusty, Mom's German Shepherd, walk in and out of my room. Mom always wanted a dog, but not just any dog. It had to be big, smart, handsome, and live up to her memory of the Alsatian that she had as a child in Poland. Rusty was all that, and more. Mom bought him when he was a puppy and cared for him as if he was her own child. She fed him the best, organic, dog food, walked him every morning, sent him to doggie camp every afternoon, and showered him with unbridled love and care. She was also strict with him, and even yelled occasionally when he disobeyed her, but after a moment or two she would be hugging and petting him and giving into his nagging for treats. It reminded me of when I was a kid.

Rusty gave my parents something to occupy their time with, since they were both retired and at home most of the time. He made sure Mom walked for 45 minutes every day, and got Dad to drive him to and from camp, morning and afternoon. He made sure they always had something to talk about, and gave them the opportunity to love and care for another living thing. He brought out their soft and sensitive side, even when times were tough. He comforted Mom and cried with her, when she was sick. He enriched Mom's final years, and was a true blessing for her.

I don't know what the mystics and philosophers say about animals having souls, but it's clear from the Bible and the Talmud that animals can serve as divine messengers. I believe that Rusty was sent to this world with a mission that he dutifully fulfilled, and continues to fulfill with my dad.

They say that dogs have the mental capacity of three year old children. If that's true then Rusty probably didn't understand the meaning of illness and death, but he seemed to know that something was wrong. Perhaps it was because he hadn't seen his master for a few days. Every time the garage door opened he would rush to see if she had returned home. Usually an extremely active, boisterous dog, Rusty was noticeably subdued. On several occasions during those last few days, he sat quietly next to me on my bed and let me stroke him as I sobbed. He sensed my sadness and the sorrow that filled the house.

When I brought Natalie home from the airport, on Thursday morning July 2nd, Dad was already on his way to the hospital. When I called him a couple of hours later he sounded upbeat. Mom was awake and eating breakfast. We rushed to see her.

Mom was so happy to see both of us. We all cried. Although she was extremely weak and exhausted, she was mentally alert and herself. She apologized to Natalie for being ill and not looking her best, and for causing her to have to leave her work and travel to America without notice. Then she thanked her profusely for coming, and told her that everything she possessed was for us to have. It was a heartbreaking moment. I can't count how many times during my lifetime Mom would tell me that everything she worked for and everything she possessed was for me to have one day. This time was different. It was real.

We stayed by her side the entire day. Family came to visit and Mom was able to speak to them, when she was awake. When she slept, I was terrified she wouldn't wake up again. When she woke, my heart leaped with joy and I celebrated by exhaling the breath I had been holding while she slept.

Natalie spent most of the time reciting Psalms near Mom's bed. The Book of Psalms is a collection of 150 liturgical poems and supplications composed, according to Jewish tradition, by King David. Psalms were sung in the ancient Jewish temple in Jerusalem, and comprise a large portion of the Jewish prayer service.

The Psalms, King David's personal supplications and praises, are infused with spiritual and mystical significance. When reciting them the supplicant enlists the support of King David to help him express his deepest emotions when he cannot find the words to do so on his own.

Jews have always recited Psalms, in their most joyous occasions and in their darkest times. This was one of our darkest moments, so we turned to the Psalms to help us cry out. I think Natalie recited the entire book many times during Mom's final week. I'm certain that her prayers reached their intended destination. They definitely brought us some measure of comfort.

CHAPTER 17

IS ANYONE LISTENING?

"Why does God not hear our prayers?" is a question everyone has, at some point, asked. The simple answer is that God does hear our prayers, but doesn't always grant us our requests. This answer is tenable in cases where our requests are not in line with the principles of ethics and morality. If we ask God for a winning hand in the casino, we can understand why we might not get a positive response, since we probably shouldn't be spending our time and money gambling. Requests for material excess are also usually understood as undeserving of divine intervention. The dilemma arises when we ask God for health, food, shelter, the basics required for survival. If God is compassionate and merciful, how can He deny these fundamentally good requests?

The answer lies in our ability, or inability, to determine absolute "good". Our field of vision is limited to what we see happening before us and what already occurred in the past. It is impossible for us to know the effect our actions will have in the future, or even in the present, on the world beyond the limits of our vision. Here's an example to illustrate this idea. You are running late to catch your flight to visit a sick relative. You beg

God to get you to the airport on time so that you can perform this good deed. You run up to the gate just as the plane doors shut. You're upset, angry. Why didn't God listen to your prayer and help you perform a good deed? An hour later you find out the plane crashed. Now you understand.

Events rarely play out with such clear cause and effect. You probably will never know what could have happened to you had you boarded that plane. Perhaps you would have gotten run over by a car at your destination but, due to your delay, the drunk driver smashed into a parked car instead. The owner of that parked car might have been unsuccessfully trying to sell it because he desperately needed money for an operation, and now would receive the exact amount necessary from the insurance payment. The drunk driver might have avoided going to jail, since he only hit a parked car, and would be able to continue supporting his wife and two kids, who would otherwise have been left without any form of support.

The exponential effects of every action in the universe at every moment are incalculable. I doubt that there is sufficient computing power in existence to even attempt it. Only an omnipotent and omnipresent force can run the world in a way that ensures that every action and occurrence is for "good". This is the secret behind the mystery of why bad things happen to good people, and vice versa. There is no objective "bad", only the appearance of "bad" within the limited vision of Man. God is good, and all his actions are good.

Accepting that everything happens for the good does not preclude us from being upset or sad when things don't go our way. We can only react to what we can perceive and comprehend. It does preclude us from becoming depressed and losing hope.

I recently read about an eighty year old retired German civil servant who has been identified as having served as a concentration camp guard directly responsible for the murder of hundreds of people. Trying and convicting him would be symbolically significant, but practically irrelevant due to his advanced age. This murderer and hundreds, perhaps thousands, of ex-Nazi murderers who were never punished for their crimes have lived happy and peaceful lives while the blood and ashes of their victims cry out for justice. Just thinking about this perverse injustice infuriates me. Without my belief in God's ultimate justice I could not bear to continue living in a world where the innocent are slaughtered and the slaughterers rewarded. But I do believe that God's justice is perfect and that the perpetrators of evil will receive the punishment they deserve, in this world or in the afterlife. This belief is what gives me the strength to overcome obstacles and deal with challenges. It is what allowed me to hope for Mom's recovery and accept that she might not recover.

CHAPTER 18

SHABBAT

On Friday, July 3rd, Mom was stable enough to be moved from the intensive care unit to a hospital room in the oncology wing. Natalie arranged for us to stay in a special room reserved for families, just a few doors from Mom, for *Shabbat*.

Shabbat, the Jewish Sabbath, begins at sundown on Friday and ends at nightfall on Saturday. Jewish law prohibits all creative activity on *Shabbat*, including switching electricity on or off and traveling in a motor vehicle. The hospital, and a Jewish chaplain who knew me and Mom, were most helpful in expediting our arrangements.

Natalie and I went food shopping with my aunt. I got my hair cut. We prepared what we feared could be our last opportunity to celebrate *Shabbat* with Mom. This would actually be the first time that we would celebrate *Shabbat* together. On our visits to my parents we never stayed with them for *Shabbat*, because they lived out of walking distance to a synagogue. Mom was always happy for us to spend *Shabbat* with friends, as long as she could have us for the rest of the week. It was heartbreaking that the one time we finally could be together was under such sad circumstances.

Shabbat is a time of rejoicing and we were determined to make this one as uplifting as possible, despite the circumstances. We began the *Shabbat* with candle lighting. Since lighting candles is prohibited in the hospital, the chaplain provided us with electric candle sticks, which according to strict Jewish law are as good as candles for fulfilling the ritual. Lighting *Shabbat* candles, traditionally a woman's obligation, symbolizes bringing peace and happiness into the home. It is considered a particularly auspicious time to pray for health and sustenance. Natalie lit candles with Mom and prayed with her.

Natalie and I recited the *Kabbalat Shabbat* prayer service, welcoming the *Shabbat*, as Mom and Dad looked on emotionally. I sang most of the prayers, including the melody I learned from the Vasloy Rebbe. I sang and prayed as I had never prayed before. The words emanating from my mouth celebrated the Sabbath Queen, but the voice emanating from my soul cried out for a miraculous salvation. It was difficult for me to hold back my tears. Sometimes I couldn't.

After prayers I recited *Kiddush*, the blessing over wine (I used grape juice) that proclaims the holiness of the day, and we all drank. Natalie had cooked soup, fish, and rice especially for Mom. It was the first, and only, time she ever cooked for Mom, since Mom would never let anyone cook in her kitchen when she was well. I think Mom would have enjoyed cooking with Natalie and I know she looked forward to teaching her all of her culinary techniques and recipes. She occasionally answered Natalie's culinary queries over the phone. Mom had an old, worn, little book filled with her handwritten recipes for her famous delicacies, in Polish, that she refused to share with anyone. She promised Natalie that she would translate them for her, but she never had the chance. Natalie's cooking reminds me a lot of Mom's. It must be their common Polish-Jewish heritage. I'll take a pass on the calf's feet.

As Mom, with great difficulty, tasted Natalie's soup there was a moment of nervous anticipation. We waited for the verdict. Drum roll. She liked it. I know my Mom, and I can tell when she's trying to be nice or when she actually means it. She meant it. She finished all of the soup and made great efforts to eat the fish and rice even though she was extremely weak. She didn't want to make her daughter-in-law feel bad.

That Friday night with my parents and my wife was the most emotional one I have ever experienced. We transformed a hospital room thick with the air of illness into a holy place filled with love and hope. There was no rejoicing that night, but there was a deep sense of gratitude to God for giving us the opportunity to spend *Shabbat* together for what we all knew would probably be our last time.

When we said goodnight to Mom she was nervous about being in the room alone for the night. She was afraid of dying alone. It was a big hospital. She was immobile, a prisoner of her bed. What would happen if something went wrong? Would the nurses know? Would she spend her final moments alone, in the dark, helpless? It must be a terrifying thought, especially for a woman who always fought for her rights and personal independence. I reassured her that her room was directly opposite the nurses' station and that they could see inside without even getting up. I also reminded her that we were sleeping just three doors from her and would be at her side if necessary. This put her at ease. It also gave me some peace of mind. I didn't want her to die alone.

CHAPTER 19

FINAL WORDS

We prayed the *Shabbat* morning service in Mom's room. Her condition was stable. The delicate procedure the doctors were performing to balance the fluids in Mom's body was working. The doctors had given her no chance of surviving, and yet she was with us, speaking, eating, thinking, watching.

I knew that her time was limited. Her liver had stopped functioning. Yet there were bits of good news. A day earlier her kidneys had appeared to be shutting down too, but today we were informed that they were working again. Her blood pressure was normal. My heart jumped with every positive word, every hopeful sign. Maybe there will be a miracle, and her liver will rejuvenate? The doctor said it was possible for the liver to come back to life on its own. Extremely unlikely, but possible. That was my opening, my basis for hope, my strength to keep from totally giving up and breaking down.

The medication Mom was taking was not successful in slowing down the Hepatitis virus that caused her liver failure. The only medical treatment for liver failure is a liver transplant, which her cancer history and treatment precluded her from. She could not survive without a functioning liver. I knew that. But a person of faith must never give up hope.

That night, after Dad had gone home, Mom became unusually alert and cogent in a way I had not seen since before her illness. She began reciting a poem in Polish. Mom spoke Polish to me since I was a child so I am conversant in the language on a rudimentary level. She recited the poem quickly and the words were difficult for me to understand, but I did catch the opening line which served as the refrain: "Death, death is no joke." It was a long poem. I marveled at how she could remember it, and I recalled how her mother had recited poems in Polish, Russian, and French in her final years. I've searched long and hard, but still haven't been able to find the poem. I hope one day I will.

Mom looked at me, then at Natalie, for a long time. She told us that she knew she was dying and that she wasn't afraid. She wanted to know that I was taken care of. Natalie put her arms around me and told her not to worry, that she would take care of me. I could see from Mom's expression that she was reassured. She told Natalie that she wanted her to have all of her things, especially her jewelry. Natalie said that she would keep the jewelry for her future children so that they would know their grandmother. She said that she would buy them things as gifts from their grandmother. Mom was satisfied.

Then Mom said, "What will happen to my husband? I love him so much. He is everything to me. What will he do? Who will take care of him? He will be all alone." We told her that we would look after Dad and that we were planning to move to America to be near him. Natalie promised to cook for him. We promised her that she need not worry. She accepted our words, and appeared reassured and at peace.

Mom knew she was dying. She accepted her fate and was done fighting. It was time for her to get her affairs in order. She couldn't move on to the next world without knowing that her loved ones were taken care of. This had been her job, and she was not one to leave a job uncompleted. She needed to know that she could leave without worry or guilt. When we gave her those assurances, we gave her the permission to move along on her journey with peace of mind. This is important for family members to recognize when dealing with a loved one who is dying. Those dying need to know that they can leave without feeling like they are abandoning their loved ones or leaving them unable to fend for themselves. Family members must clearly and strongly reassure them, giving them permission to continue their journey in peace.

Mom was probably also evaluating her life. The thought of evaluating my own life terrifies me. Did I use my time wisely or did I waste it? Did I treat people with respect and kindness or did I ignore or insult them? I imagine being forced to watch a movie of my life, everything I ever did or even thought, right before my eyes.

I'm reminded of the time, in my early twenties, when I received a call from a girl that I had wanted to date, but who just wanted to be friends. I had said some not nice things about her to a very close buddy of mine, who happened to know her too, assuming that it was totally confidential. He told her what I said (he, of course, denied doing so) and she called me on it. It's been over twenty years, but I still remember my stomach dropping to the floor and the feeling of nausea and shame engulfing me as she rebuked me on the phone. I had nothing to say in my defense, no excuse to offer, just apologies and shame. It was one of the worst five minutes I've ever experienced. It is that same feeling magnified and multiplied hundreds, perhaps thousands, of times, that I fear will overtake me again as I watch the film of my life.

According to many rabbinic commentators, this feeling of intense shame constitutes what is referred to as *Gehinnom*, or Hell. Our evil deeds become our punishment in the afterlife by afflicting our souls with unbearable shame. That instance of clarity, when we view our lives, the choices we made, and the deeds we committed in the context of absolute and eternal truth and justice, is both our punishment and our purification. The more spiritual and righteous the life, the less pain and shame endured. For those who have perpetrated unspeakable evil, the torment is unbearable and eternal.

Maimonides, the preeminent medieval rabbinic scholar, advised every person to evaluate their actions each day, as if it were their last day on earth. That way they would be certain to live each day as meaningfully and righteously as possible.

On his death bed, the Chassidic master Reb Zusya said, "In the World to Come, they will not ask me, why were you not Moses? They will ask me, why were you not Zusya?" All we can hope, or be expected, to do in this world is to fulfill our true potential.

I reassured Mom that she had been a great mother. I felt she needed to hear that from me because she always thought I didn't appreciate her. Sure we had our differences over the years including lots of screaming matches and "I hate yous", just like any other mother and child team, but I never stopped loving and appreciating her.

I thanked her for giving me the gift of a Jewish education, even during several financially trying years when we could not afford the tuition. It would have made sense to pull me out of *yeshiva* and send me to the perfectly good public school in our suburban town. Mom insisted that I remain in *yeshiva*, although it meant asking for a scholarship and revealing our dismal financial condition to strangers, something that was undoubtedly excruciating for her. I don't exactly know why she did it. It might have been because she wanted me to have a Jewish education, or because she didn't like the idea of her little boy being in a school where he would be exposed to sex, drugs, and all the other wonderful influences that are prevalent in our modern, progressive public school system. I think the real reason was that she knew I loved *yeshiva* and that I was thriving there academically and socially. My happiness was more important to her than anything, even her personal pride.

I reminded her of how she drove me the half hour to *yeshiva* every morning and how she made sure I had kosher food to eat at home. I told her that she got the credit for me becoming a rabbi and for all the people I've helped and all the Torah I've taught, and that she would continue receiving the merit of all of my deeds.

I reassured her that she had led a meaningful and fulfilling life. She built a loving family, had many friends and social relationships, and was a respected member of her community. I know that she took my words seriously and gained comfort from knowing that she was going on her journey fortified with Jewish religious merit, since she sincerely believed in God and was proud of her Jewish heritage and tradition.

Throughout that day several of her old friends came to visit, but she was always asleep, unable to be woken. After they would leave she would, surprisingly, awaken. It was obvious to me that she did not want to deal with visitors other than her own family. She didn't want to hear empty words of encouragement, or waste her time with small talk. She wanted to use all of her remaining energy to prepare for death. Even the mention of her dear Rusty barely evoked a response from her. Of course she loved the dog, but he was only a dog, an animal. She needed to concern herself with people, her loved ones. She had entered a state of higher consciousness as she prepared to transition to a spiritual world of absolute truth and clarity.

She grew silent and stared at me for a long time. Her eyes began to shine, as if she was gazing through me at something beautiful. I imagine it was her blonde little boy, Arnie, whom she cherished with all her heart, now a man that she could be proud of, that she was lovingly admiring. As she always said, I was her everything, her reason for existing, her pride and joy, her life. I was her greatest accomplishment, her fulfillment.

In the days and weeks prior, I suspect she was angry at her predicament. Why did this have to happen to her when she had so much to live for? She had finally sold her business and now had the time to enjoy life. Her son was married to a wonderful girl that she loved, and soon there would be the grandchildren for whom she had been waiting for so many years. This was her time to shine, her golden years, and they were being stolen from her while she lay helpless, unable to fight. On that Saturday night, as she spoke with her children, she gave up her anger and made peace with her life.

She began humming the melodies to some of the pieces that I played on the piano as a child. Fur Elise. Rondo Alla Turca. Mom loved the piano, although she never learned to play. Her mother was an accomplished pianist, having studied in a music conservatory in Warsaw, and she loved listening to her play. Mom arranged for me to take piano lessons from when I was around nine years old until sixteen. She made sure that I practiced for one hour a day, every day. I hated practicing and often pleaded with Mom to go easy on me, but she stood firm and promised that one day I would thank her. I'm still not sure that I agree with her method, but I do play pretty well today, so . . . thanks Mom.

I then sang the lively Israeli folk songs that Mom sang to me when I was a child. She seemed to enjoy them. Perhaps they reminded her of her younger days as a vivacious teenager, ready to conquer the world. She faded into sleep. I said goodnight, recited the *Shema*, and blessed her.

I was overwhelmed with awe and respect. I had just witnessed a human being, my mother, preparing for death. She wasn't afraid. She was calm, collected, and fully aware. She needed to know that her life was in order so that she could leave. When I assured her that her life had been meaningful and that her loved ones would be cared for, she became peaceful. She could sing songs and relive happy memories, as she began the transition to her next life. This is the way the righteous leave this world. I was so proud of her, proud to be her son.

CHAPTER 20

SECOND CHANCE

I've always felt uneasy in hospitals. They are a blessing that, unless you are a woman in labor, you don't wish even on your enemies. I've never been a patient in a hospital, but I spent a lot of time in one when my grandmother was ill. I was around eleven years old when she was diagnosed with a malignant cancer of the esophagus. The cancer was successfully removed, but a day or two after the operation she had a stroke which left her left side paralyzed. All this was happening in Montreal, where my grandparents lived. Almost every weekend, my parents and I would drive the seven hours from New Jersey to visit. Mom and I stayed in Montreal for an entire summer. Mom stayed another summer without me.

We spent the next year in hospitals, convalescent homes, and finally helping my grandmother manage in her own home. My grandfather never left her side. Despite her confinement to a wheelchair and her slightly affected mental capabilities, she was still essentially the same woman we all loved and respected. She continued to recite poetry in French, Russian, and Polish, and her greatest dream was to live to see me become a *Bar Mitzvah* (age 13). She made it. Throughout it all Mom worked tirelessly for grandmother. She was an extraordinary daughter. Her dedication to her mother left a deep and lasting impression on me. I only hoped that I could be there in a similar way for her.

I returned to the hospital the next day, Sunday, hopeful that Mom would be as awake and alert as she had been the night before. She was awake for a short time early in the day, but as the day wore on, she slept more and more. When her friends came to visit, she could not be woken. The doctor told us that she was falling into the hepatic coma, which would eventually become permanent. Everyone was giving up hope, including Dad. I refused to give up. I sat next to her, leaned close to her face, and spoke to her. I begged her to wake up. We needed her. It was not her time yet. It was too soon. She did not respond. I became more forceful. I demanded, loudly, that she open her eyes and speak with us.

I closed my eyes and visualized her soul. I called out to it. I visualized Mom's parents and asked them to help her wake up. I described what I was doing, for Mom to hear. When I mentioned my grandmother I could see the slightest movement of her eyelids. I visualized myself holding a pale of cold water and pouring it on Mom. Still no response. I finally told Mom that she had to wake up to speak with Natalie. Her daughter-in-law had traveled so far to be with her and would be hurt if her mother-in-law left without speaking with her.

Mom opened her eyes. It seemed like a miracle. I cried with joy and immediately called Dad to let him speak with her. It was as if Mom had come back from the other world. She had, what appeared to me as, an annoyed look on her face, as if I had dragged her from her peaceful destination back to her painful reality. She had made peace with her life and her death the night before, and now I was telling her that her business in this world was not yet completed. I needed her. I wasn't ready to say goodbye. Mom fought with all the energy she had left to return and give me one last chance to say goodbye.

CHAPTER 21

HOSPICE

Mom refused to eat. When the nurse attempted to feed her she stubbornly clamped her mouth shut. We assumed that her loss of appetite was due to her condition. We found out the real reason when a hospice representative came to speak with us.

Modern conventional medicine advocates treating a patient until it is no longer physically possible to do so, even if the prognosis for the patient is terminal. The only exception is when the patient specifically declines to be sustained by artificial respiration. If the patient has not left clear instructions, the next of kin decides whether or not to place the patient on a respirator.

Hospice care accepts that death is the natural course that everyone must take, and advocates letting terminal patients die peacefully and with respect, in as much comfort and in as little pain as possible. Accordingly, when doctors determine that there is no medical chance of survival, all intrusive procedures and tests are discontinued and pain medication is provided as needed. Hospice care can be administered in the patient's home or in a medical facility.

When we were asked to decide whether to place Mom under hospice care, my initial reaction was to resist. How could we give up on her? Shouldn't we keep trying to keep her alive at all costs? The hospice representative, an experienced hospice nurse, explained to us that Mom was actively dying. She had accepted her fate and made peace with it. She was ready to leave the hospital, her doctors and nurses, and her weak, swollen, incapacitated body behind, and move on to the better place that she believed awaited her. This is why she refused to eat or to communicate anymore. She had consciously decided to stop fighting and to start dying. We respected her wish and agreed to place her under hospice care.

The implication of hospice devastated me. It forced me to accept that Mom was dying, but I refused to view it as a declaration of hopelessness and loss of faith. If a miracle was meant to occur, then it would happen under any circumstance. Cessation of medical treatment was irrelevant. I never stopped hoping for a miracle, but I also accepted the reality of death and the role it plays in human life.

Death is not evil. It is simply the final chapter of every person's book of life. We all must, will, experience it. There is no ultimate escape, only temporary stays. All we can hope for is the chance to die peacefully, at peace with ourselves and those we love. We had done everything in our power to give Mom life. Now we had to make the same effort to give her the chance to leave peacefully and painlessly. This was the hardest decision I've ever had to make, but I know it was the right one. I have no regrets.

On Monday, July 6th, Mom was moved into a private room down the hall from where she had been. Her vital signs were monitored and pain medication was administered. No more pills, blood tests, or intrusive examinations and procedures. Just as much comfort and peace as possible.

As I write these words I realize that I completely missed the fourth of July holiday weekend. In my world there was no independence or celebration, just sadness, stress, worry, and pain.

CHAPTER 22

BETWEEN LIFE AND DEATH

Monday, July 7th. Mom could no longer speak. When her eyes were open she would sometimes look at me. Mostly she would gaze straight ahead. I don't know what she was looking at, if she could even focus. I think she was still able to see me that morning, but from then on she had a glassy, fixed stare, which is considered to be one of the signs of dying. Mom seemed to be unconscious even though her eyes were open, but I believe that she could hear everything going on around her. Natalie and I continued speaking to her, reassuring her that we were taken care of and that we loved her.

There are many documented cases of people who awoke from comas and remembered things that had been said in their presence. The spirit, or soul, is awake even when the body is not. As a person moves closer to death, and the body gets weaker, the soul comes to the fore and takes on a more prominent role, no longer constrained by the shackles of the physical. Mom's soul was gradually separating from her body. I could feel her soul's presence in the room. I could feel it finding comfort in the Psalms and prayers Natalie and I continued to recite throughout the day.

Tuesday was not much different than Monday. Mom was fading away. Her eyes were now totally glazed over. Her mouth was open most of the time, but her breathing was still relatively steady and peaceful. Occasionally she would moan, as a result of acid reflux. The nurse increased her pain medication. The main thing now was for her to be as comfortable as possible. I didn't want her to suffer anymore.

Wednesday was another day. More prayers and tears. Mom's breathing was regular and her eyes were open, but she was somewhere else. I still believed that she could hear us, so I continued speaking to her.

Prayer is an amazing, God given gift that allows us to affect ourselves, our world, and even our destiny. Along with that power come the consequences of our actions. What we see as beneficial could turn out detrimental in the long term. Therefore, in cases where our judgment might be faulty, we should pray for the "right thing" to happen instead of our desired outcome. Praying for health and healing is clearly always the right thing, but accepting death as part of our natural destiny also has its place.

The Talmud recounts that when Rabbi Judah the Prince, the greatest of the rabbinic sages of his day, was suffering greatly from a terminal illness all of the sages gathered at his home to pray for him. Their prayers prevented his death but could not affect a cure or ease his suffering. Rabbi Judah's maidservant, seeing that he continued to suffer, prayed that "the celestial beings should overcome the earth-dwellers (the sages)." In other words, she prayed that her master be spared more suffering and be allowed to die. When she realized that her prayer was being overpowered by those of the sages, she distracted the sages by breaking a vase, causing them to momentarily stop praying. It was during that momentary pause that Rabbi Judah died. The message is clear: sometimes death is the "right thing".

The intention behind my prayers changed. A few days earlier I had prayed for a miraculous recovery, for Mom's liver to spontaneously rejuvenate, for the virus to be defeated. True, the odds were heavily stacked against us, but to believers in divine intervention, probability and statistics are interesting, but irrelevant. Since Mom was moved to hospice, I felt that praying just for recovery was unrealistic.

My faith prevented me from dismissing the possibility of a miracle, but the reality of seeing Mom slowly leave this world and my desire to protect her from further suffering forced me to reframe my request to God. I prayed, "Master of the World, if it is Your will to have mercy on Mom and save her, then please do so now, but if You have decreed that it is her time to leave this world, then please end her suffering and take her into Your arms quickly and peacefully. Don't keep all of us in this state of limbo, suspended between life and death, unable to rejoice or mourn."

At night, before leaving, I recited the evening prayers and said the *Shema* for Mom. I then turned on the two *Shabbat* candle lamps that we had been given by the chaplain. Even though it wasn't *Shabbat*, I felt it was significant to have a light kindled near Mom. According to Jewish tradition there is a deep connection between a candle or lamp, and the soul. The Book of Proverbs says, "The candle of God is the soul of man." The flame of a candle is ephemeral, it has no mass, no weight, yet its light can fill up a room, give off heat, and dazzle the eye. A flame always rises up, even if held upside down. I hoped that the *Shabbat* lights would help uplift and strengthen Mom's soul.

CHAPTER 23

A FINAL BLESSING

Thursday, July 9th corresponded to the seventeenth day of the Hebrew month of Tammuz. On this day in the year seventy of the Common Era, the Roman Legions lead by Titus breached the walls of Jerusalem after a long siege. Three weeks later, on the ninth day of the Hebrew month of Av, they destroyed the holy Jewish Temple. Both days are commemorated with fasting and gestures of mourning. The fast of the seventeenth of Tammuz marks the beginning of a three week period of national mourning that culminates on the ninth of Av. This three week period is considered to be a time of bad *mazel*, or luck, when tragedies are more apt to occur than at any other time of the year. I felt this negative energy in a very real way.

Mom's mouth was now open all the time and her breathing was labored, as if she was fighting for each breath. It was painful for me to watch. It reminded me of the day my grandmother died. She was at home, sitting in her wheelchair, her mouth open, struggling for each breath of air. I remember sitting next to her, speaking to her, touching her, but she could not respond in words, just with her gaze. Hours later, lying in her bed, with

Mom, Dad, grandfather, and me close to her, she passed away. Her skin was yellow, as a result of the hepatitis virus that attacked her liver. She was 72 years old. Now I watched Mom, her skin yellow, her mouth open, 72 years old. I knew the end was near.

I don't recall if I fasted that day. I think I did for most of the day, but sundown, marking the end of the fast, was around 9:00pm and I needed to keep up my strength at Mom's bedside. Mom fasted, perhaps for the first time on the seventeenth of Tammuz.

I was scared later that night. I wanted to be by Mom's side for as long as possible. I didn't want her to be alone when her time came to leave this world. But it was late, time to go home. As I write these words I wonder why I didn't just stay. Hospice rules specifically permitted one person to spend the night in a patient's room. So what if it was late? So what if I spent one uncomfortable night on a recliner in Mom's room? Maybe I thought that Mom wouldn't have wanted me to inconvenience myself and stay. She probably wouldn't have. Maybe I thought I would be more useful after a good night's sleep at home. I don't know. I wish I had stayed with Mom through the night, but I didn't.

As had become my normal practice, I recited the evening prayers at Mom's bedside. Before leaving, I noticed that one of the *Shabbat* lights I had lit the previous night had extinguished. I knew it was a sign. A soul was preparing to return to the Master of Souls. I recited the *Shema*, the ultimate Jewish declaration of faith in one God, at Mom's side for what I felt would be the last time. As I said those ancient, sacred words, I silently added my own prayers.

Shema Yisrael, Adon-ai Elohe-ynu Adon-ai Echad – Hear Israel, the Lord is our God, the Lord is One.

Please God, accept Mom's soul like the souls of all the holy martyrs who sanctified Your Name with their final breaths by declaring their unbending faith in You.

Blessed be the name of His glorious kingdom forever.

Our prophets have taught us that this is how the angels bless You. Let Mom dwell among those angels in heaven.

Love the Lord your God with all your heart, with all your soul, and with all of your means.

When the great Jewish sage Rabbi Akiva was being martyred by the Romans he chanted this prayer. When he reached the words "with all your soul", he smiled and remarked that he never thought he would have the chance to fulfill the meaning of these words, until now. He died at that moment. May You accept Mom's soul as you did Rabbi Akiva's.

These words which I command you today shall be in your heart, and you shall teach them to your children and speak about them when you are at home and when you travel, when you lay down to sleep and when you awake.

Remember that Mom always believed in You from the depths of her heart, and imparted her faith to me. She sacrificed so that I could study your Torah and become a rabbi. Give her the reward she deserves.

I then blessed her with the traditional Priestly blessing:

"May God bless you and keep you.
May God cause the divine light to shine upon you and be
gracious to you.
May God turn His face toward you, and grant you peace."

I said, "I love you, Mom," and left the room with a heavy heart. As Natalie and I waited for the elevator I said, "I feel that this might be the last time we ever see Mom, with us, again."

Mom with her parents in post WWII Poland.

Mom in Poland, mid-1950's.

Mom's father, Elimelech Rajner, (top) in Polish army uniform
wearing medal of valor and (bottom) seated.

Wedding photo of (L-R) Author, Natalie, Mom, and Dad. Taken Sept. 1, 2008.

(L-R) Mom, Natalie, and Natalie's mom before ceremony.

(L-R) Rachela and Mom at Wedding.

Enjoying the Wedding.

Mom - 1961

Mom and Author at Wedding.

Mom and Author 1967

Yehuda Singer at 2 Months.

PART II

CHAPTER 1

PASSING

I answered the phone at 5:15am on Friday, July 10th, 2009. The nurse informed me that my mother, Jeane Singer, Yehudit daughter of Elimelech, passed away moments earlier. My world collapsed around me. I turned to Natalie; "she's gone". I had to tell my father. He was in bed. I'm not sure if the phone had woken him. I went to his side and put my hand on his shoulder. I tried not to cry. I failed. "Dad, Mom is...I'm so sorry...," my voice trembled. I cried. He let loose a loud cry, like I never heard him do before. He ran into the bathroom to shower. I continued to hear his cries. We dressed and rushed to the hospital.

We walked into Mom's room. She was lying on the bed in the fetal position with her eyes opened, untouched. She looked so small, her body emaciated, a shell of her former self, the energy and life force sucked out of her. How can I attempt to describe how I felt seeing my mother lying there, lifeless? I can't, I won't. There are no words. She was gone. She was finally at peace.

It is at these times of intense emotional pain and sorrow, when we are paralyzed with grief and unable to think clearly, that religious tradition and ritual enter to provide us with direction, structure, and meaning. Judaism has detailed rules and traditions covering every minute aspect relating to death and mourning. I relied on these to help me function at a time when all I wanted to do was crawl into a dark room, alone, and sob.

I had always avoided studying the laws of mourning because I believed that doing so would draw the attention of the Angel of Death, based on the Talmudic statement, "Do not initiate a conversation with Satan." I would study them when necessary. The time had come, and I didn't know what to do. I called my good friend of nearly two decades, Rabbi Mark Wildes, and we discussed what I needed to do, and when the funeral would take place.

According to Jewish law, the burial must take place as soon as possible, preferably on the day of death. It is considered disrespectful for the deceased and a torment for the soul to leave the corpse unburied. Only under extenuating circumstances may the burial be postponed. Even though it was a Friday, and the approach of the Sabbath could preclude burial, since sundown wasn't until around 8:00pm, Rabbi Wildes recommended that the funeral and burial take place that same afternoon.

It would seem that the sensible thing would have been to postpone the funeral to Sunday, to give us more time to inform people and allow them to plan their schedules. But that would have gone against Jewish law and tradition. Mom's soul was now in a place where religious tradition reigned supreme. I felt strongly that following that tradition would bring peace to her soul and honor to her memory. Moreover, I couldn't bear the thought of living another two days knowing that Mom's body was lying in a funeral home. Her body needed to return to the earth, as God said to Adam in the Book of Genesis, "For you are dust, and to dust you shall return."

I called the funeral home, which happened to be across the street from the hospital, and made arrangements for them to pick up Mom's body. Just verbalizing Mom's death, saying "My mother died", caused me to break down in tears. I could barely get the words out. I needed Natalie to help me get through the call.

I turned my attention to Mom. Her eyes needed to be closed. The Zohar, the primary Jewish mystical text, states that the deceased can see in the next world only after her eyes are closed in this world. As much as I dreaded it, I felt that I should be the one to do it. It was my duty to honor her in life, and now in death. I placed my hand on her, and with trepidation, gently closed her eyes. I then covered her with a sheet, from head to toe. It was the last time I would ever see Mom's body.

I opened a window, which according to tradition represents the soul leaving the body and ascending to the heavens. This should be viewed metaphorically, since the soul is a purely spiritual creation with no physical dimensions. Similarly, the Talmud states that one should only pray in a structure with windows which, when feasible, are opened to allow the prayers to rise to the heavens.

I think the meaning behind this idea of open windows facilitating spiritual elevation is directed at the worshiper or participant rather than the actual soul or prayer. The open window forces us to look beyond ourselves and our sheltered environment into a vast, unknown world which we are part of, but can never control or even fully comprehend. We recognize our relative insignificance, but rejoice in our ability to connect with and become part of an even greater spiritual world surrounding us, yet just beyond our field of vision. Our physical selves may be confined by the boundaries of nature, environment, and the barriers we erect, but our souls cannot be constrained from reaching the heights they naturally strive towards.

The funeral director arrived. When possible, only Jews should handle the deceased. Since the director was not Jewish, Dad and I lifted Mom's body from the bed onto a stretcher and accompanied it to the transport.

At the funeral home we met with the director to make the necessary arrangements. The cemetery where Mom would be buried was in Toms River, NJ, an hour and half drive from the funeral home down the Garden State Parkway South. As it was a Friday in July and people would be heading towards the shore for the weekend causing heavy traffic delays, the funeral director strongly suggested, practically insisted, that the funeral be postponed until Sunday. Our initial reaction was to follow the director's instructions. I called Rabbi Wildes. He told me that the right thing to do was to conduct the funeral and burial today, regardless of the traffic threat, and that I should be firm with the funeral director. It was his job to fulfill our request regardless of the inconvenience it might cause him. I told the director that the funeral had to be done today. We agreed upon twelve noon, which would give us enough time to get to Toms River and back well before the Sabbath.

We made phone calls to inform family and friends. I got through a few. Natalie made most of them. I posted a notice on Facebook and sent out an email. Thanks to technology and the internet, the word spread. Most of our family and Mom's friends lived in the area, so attending the funeral on short notice was feasible. Rabbi Wildes agreed to officiate.

Chapter 2

Preparation

The Jewish laws of mourning apply to the loss of a parent, spouse, child, and sibling. From the moment of death until burial the mourner is called an *Onen*. An *Onen* is exempt from reciting prayers and blessings, and from performing most positive religious obligations because he is assumed to be overwhelmed with grief and preoccupied with making arrangements for the care of the deceased. All the standard laws of mourning, that will soon be described, apply as well.

Not reciting prayers or blessings may sound trivial, but to an observant Jew it is disorienting. Since my *bar mitzvah* I've missed reciting the morning prayers only a handful of times, due to severe illness. Jewish law recognizes that the death of a loved one is disorienting, shocking, and often paralyzing. One can think of nothing else besides one's immense loss. There is simply not enough mental or emotional room to do anything else. Any energy remaining must be focused on honoring the deceased by arranging for their care and burial. I temporarily lost the ability to focus on the religious obligations that have been the mainstay of my life. All I could think of was Mom's death and burial.

We arrived at the funeral chapel. I was asked to identify Mom. I followed the funeral director to a back room. The simple, unadorned, wooden casket lay before me. This type of casket is prescribed by Jewish tradition for it accentuates the supremacy of the spirit over the adornments of the physical and acknowledges that material possessions have no value in the spiritual world of eternity. "For you are dust, and to dust you shall return."

The funeral director opened the casket. Mom was dressed in *Tachrichin* (Takh-ree-kheen), the traditional clean, unadorned, white, handmade linen shrouds. These shrouds symbolize purity, simplicity, and dignity. They have no pockets, to represent the futility of material possessions in the eternal world of the spirit.

Mom's head was covered with a bonnet, her face with a cloth. The director revealed her face. There was a small pottery shard covering each eye, based on the mystical tradition that the soul cannot see in the afterlife until her physical eyes are covered. Her body was a shell from which her soul had been released. Interestingly, one of the Hebrew words used to describe death is *Petira,* which literally means "release". I was despondent to see her for the last time, yet I was comforted to know that we were honoring her by preparing her for her journey according to the letter of Jewish law and tradition.

Judaism considers the care of the dead body a sacred task of the highest order. The organization responsible for this task is called the *Chevra Kadisha*, the holy fraternity. The process of preparing the body for burial is called *Tahara*, which means purification. The *Tahara* may only be performed by pious Jews of the same gender as the deceased, for reasons of modesty. These men and women purify the body by pouring water over it in a particular manner, and dress it in *Tachrichim*.

Mystical tradition teaches that prior to burial, the soul of the deceased remains in the vicinity of its body looking down upon it with great pain and sorrow. It sees and hears everything around its body. In deference to this, every part of the *Tahara* process is performed with the utmost respect for the deceased. The body is never turned face down or totally uncovered. Those performing the *Tahara* mention the deceased full Hebrew name and ask for forgiveness in case they inadvertently insult or shame them during the process. Conversation, eating, and smoking are prohibited during the *Tahara*. Prayers and Psalms are recited to help elevate the soul.

The body must be accompanied or watched over by a Jew from the time of death until burial, as a sign of respect and care. While Dad and I went to the director's office to fill out forms, Natalie watched over Mom until the *Chevra Kaddisha* arrived. She told me later that it was the greatest honor she has ever been granted.

The many detailed tasks that are part of the *Tahara* process, that are beyond the scope of this book, are all concerned with respecting and honoring the deceased.

Chapter 3

Tearing

Dad and I stood in the lobby surrounded by family. Rabbi Wildes arrived with several other rabbis with whom I had worked. Many of my friends and many of Mom's old friends were there. It was a beautiful showing, particularly for such short notice, and a great show of respect. I was extremely touched and grateful.

I could barely speak more than a sentence without breaking down. My sadness was overwhelming. Rabbi Wildes approached Dad and me to perform the *Keriah*, the religiously mandated tearing of one's garment, representing our anguish and the irreversibility of death. The torn garment is worn throughout the initial seven day mourning period. In many non-orthodox settings the *Keriah* has been turned into a less intense, strictly symbolic act, by simply tearing a small black ribbon or cloth attached to the garment, thus sparing the actual garment from damage. In my opinion, this circumvents the true purpose of the ritual. How can you be concerned with a garment while your loved one lies lifeless before you? On the other hand, destroying an expensive garment is wasteful and Jewish law frowns upon unnecessary wastefulness. I struggled with this issue. I know Mom would definitely not have wanted me to tear a good suit on her account, but I felt the need to honor her by wearing a suit to her funeral, and the need to express my grief in a tangible way that would materially affect me and be visible to all. I compromised and wore a suit that was fashionable but that I rarely wore.

There is a blessing that is recited before tearing the garment:

Baruch Ata Ado-nai Elo-heynu Melech Ha-Olam Dayan Ha-Emet.

Blessed are You our God, king of the universe, the true judge.

Reciting a blessing on such a sorrowful occasion seems inappropriate but, for the mourner, it is the beginning of a slow healing process. For months I had prayed, cried, and pleaded to God for Mom's life. I stood by her side as she fought with all her might to live, and watched as she succumbed to her illness and died. I couldn't understand or explain why she had to leave this world when she had so much to live for. I had no answers. I could react with bitterness and anger at God and at the world, and let those negative feelings destroy me. Instead, I chose to accept that Mom's death was part of her destiny, the final chapter in a productive and fulfilling life. She had a mission to fulfill in this world, as we all do. Once she fulfilled her mission she could not remain in this world for even a moment longer. Only the True Judge knows our exact mission and determines when it has been fulfilled. This is the mystery of life and death. We accept this to be true by blessing the True Judge.

Rabbi Wildes tore my suit jacket lapel and my shirt several inches, and my broken heart was revealed for all to see.

CHAPTER 4

EULOGY

I often wonder how I will act in highly emotionally charged situations. Will I hold it together or break down and lose it? You never really know until it happens.

I remember my first encounter with death. Mom informed me that my great uncle Srulek had passed away. I was probably around six or seven years old. I had always enjoyed going to Uncle Srulek's house in Montreal, since he would play with me and give me treats. When Mom told me the news, I didn't react. Sometime later, when I was alone, I fell face down onto a pillow on the living room couch and sobbed. There was no preparation or warning. My tears flowed spontaneously. Even at that young age I was able to comprehend the enormity and finality of death, and it tore my little heart apart.

The first funeral I attended was my grandmother's. I was fourteen. I cried throughout the service and the burial. I didn't plan on crying. I didn't want to. I tried to hold back, but I was physically unable to stem the flow of tears. My brain was not in control of my emotions. My soul was in control, and it could not remain silent as it watched the lady I loved with all my heart depart forever.

Now, thirty years later, I sat in the front row of a funeral chapel and listened to the rabbi praise Mom's life and mourn her passing. My sorrow was greater than anything I ever felt. This was my Mom.

The purpose of a eulogy is to honor the life of the deceased. In modern Western society, most people spend their lives accumulating material possessions and striving for wealth and the social status that comes with it. I doubt that there has ever been a eulogy in which the financial success or degree of wealth of the deceased has been praised. You'll never hear, "he was a rich man", "he loved making money", "he strove to always buy the newest most expensive sports car". Nobody wants to be remembered like that. When we see death lying before us in a wooden box we understand that material possessions and wealth are no longer relevant. As the saying goes, "you can't take it with you." What you can take with you is your good name and reputation, and the good deeds you have accomplished in your lifetime. If we could only carry that understanding with us throughout life, the world would be a vastly different, and better, place. Unfortunately, we usually leave it behind at the funeral chapel or cemetery, and continue with our materialistic pursuit of happiness.

There is a parable told by the Maggid of Dubno, one of the greatest Jewish ethical teachers, that powerfully brings home this point. A poor man overheard some sailors describing an island covered with diamonds. The man told his wife about his discovery, traded his meager possessions for ship passage, and set off on the month long voyage to the mysterious island. When he disembarked, he couldn't believe his eyes. The beach was covered with diamonds. He began picking up diamonds and stuffing them in his pockets. After a few moments he stopped and realized that he needed a boat that he could fill up with diamonds to take back home.

He walked into town, entered a boat maker's shop, and asked for a boat. The boat maker was happy to serve him and inquired how the man intended to pay for the boat. The man pulled out a handful of diamonds and placed them on the counter. The boat maker laughed, "Diamonds are worthless on this island. They are everywhere. The currency on this island is fish, which is our prime means of nourishment." He told the man that a small boat would cost one thousand fish, and that he would sell him one on credit. The man thanked the boat maker, took his boat, and proceeded to learn how to fish. After several weeks of hard work and an apprenticeship with a master fisherman, the man had paid off his debt and was finally ready to begin collecting diamonds.

After so many weeks of fishing and living on the island, the man began to think like a native and associate wealth with fish. Why should he waste his time gathering worthless diamonds when real wealth lay in fish? So the man decided to buy a much larger boat and catch as many fish as possible to bring home with him and live the life of a rich man. He fished for weeks to accumulate enough fish to pay for a larger vessel. Then he fished for months and accumulated thousands of fish, which he securely stored on his ship. When he had filled his vessel, he set off on the month long journey home with his treasure.

His wife and son waited on the dock for his triumphant return. Suddenly a powerful smell assaulted their nostrils. They saw a ship approaching. The closer it got, the stronger the smell became. The ship docked and the man emerged, beaming with satisfaction. He confidently strutted towards his wife and proclaimed the success of his mission. They were rich beyond their wildest dreams. His wife asked, "What is that rotten stench coming from your boat? Where are the diamonds you went to find?" The man smirked, "Don't be foolish. Diamonds are worthless. Fish is what is truly valuable, and I have accumulated enough to make us rich beyond our wildest dreams." "You crazy old fool," she scolded. "Diamonds are precious. All you have is a ship full of worthless, rotten fish!" Reality struck the man. He realized his outrageous mistake and was devastated. He wasted all of his time on the island gathering fish instead of diamonds. As he sulked home with his wife and child he shoved a hand into his pocket and found the few diamonds that he had initially picked up on the island, with which he was able to provide for his family for the next few years.

The island in the parable represents our lives. The diamonds are good deeds. Our mission in this world is to gather as many diamonds as possible, which in the world of eternity, are extremely valuable. We quickly realize that these diamonds are worthless in this world. Material wealth, represented by fish in the parable, is what counts. So we spend our lives pursuing wealth instead of gathering diamonds. When we leave this world and return to the world of eternity we are shocked and dismayed to realize that we wasted our lives catching fish instead of gathering the diamonds.

Earlier in the day Rabbi Wildes asked me what I would like him to say about Mom. I told him that she was energetic, extremely hard working, and that she took pride in her work and in everything she did, but next to her family, everything was insignificant. Her main purpose in life was to take care of her family. She gave her husband and son everything she had, her energy, her strength, and most of all, her love. Her son was the apple of her eye, the purpose of her existence. She shared her pride in him with everyone she met. She made sure he received a Jewish education and raised him to be proud of his heritage and strong in his faith. She lived to see her prayers fulfilled and her dream come true when she walked him down the aisle to the wedding canopy and watched as he married a woman she embraced as her own daughter.

Mom did catch her share of fish, but she also accumulated a huge treasure of diamonds.

CHAPTER 5

BURIAL

After the eulogy, the rabbi recited a special prayer beginning with the words *El Maleh Rahamim* – God full of compassion. The prayer mentions the deceased by full Hebrew name and asks God to grant her eternal peace.

> **El Maleh Rahamiṇ** – *God, full of compassion, who dwells on high,*
>
> *Grant proper rest on the wings of the divine Presence,*
>
> *Among the lofty holy and pure who shine like the radiance of heaven,*
>
> *To the soul of Yehudit daughter of Elimelech who has gone to her eternal destiny, (for I pledge to give charity in her memory),*
>
> *May her eternal repose be in the Garden of Eden.*
>
> *Therefore, Master of Compassion, shelter her in Your wings forever,*
>
> *And bind her in the bond of everlasting life.*
> *The Lord is her inheritance. May she rest in peace,*
> *And let us say, Amen.*

I had recited this prayer dozens of times at funerals and in the synagogue, as part of my cantorial duties. There is nothing I wanted more than to honor Mom by chanting it at her funeral, but I knew that I couldn't. I tried numerous times in my mind. The words tore at my heart. The mention of Mom's name would unleash a wave of tears. Maybe at some point in the future. Definitely not now.

According to tradition, honoring the deceased is called the truest form of kindness, since reciprocation is not a motive. Carrying and escorting the casket is a great show of respect. Our close male relatives came forward to honor Mom by carrying her casket to the hearse. Dad, Natalie, and I followed close behind. The rest of the assembled followed us, forming a somber procession of honor, escorting a loved one on her final journey to her eternal resting place. The rabbi recited Psalm 91:

He who dwells in the shelter of the Most High Dwells in the shadow of the Almighty.

I will say to the LORD, "My refuge and my fortress, My God, in whom I trust!"

For He delivers you from the trapper's snare And from the deadly pestilence.

He will cover you with His pinions, And under His wings you may seek refuge;

His faithfulness is a shield and bulwark. You will not be afraid of the terror by night, Or of the arrow that flies by day;

Of the pestilence that stalks in darkness,
Or of the destruction that lays waste at noon.

A thousand may fall at your side
And ten thousand at your right hand,
But it shall not approach you.

You will only look on with your eyes
And see the recompense of the wicked.

For you said, "the LORD is my refuge",
You made the Most High your dwelling place.

No evil will befall you,
Nor will any plague come near your tent.

For He will command His angels concerning you,
To guard you in all your ways.

They will bear you up in their hands,
That you do not strike your foot against a stone.

You will tread upon the lion and cobra,
The young lion and the serpent you will trample.

Because he has loved Me, I will deliver him;
I will set him securely on high, because he has known My
name.

He will call upon Me, and I will answer him;
I will be with him in trouble;
I will rescue him and honor him.
With a long life I will satisfy him
And let him see My salvation."

The Toms River Jewish Cemetery is where my paternal grandparents are buried. My grandfather died in 1962, my grandmother in 2000 at age 102. The family long since moved from Toms River, but their connection to the cemetery remains. If it was up to me I would have a chosen a cemetery closer to where we all live, but it was Dad's decision. He purchased a double plot, so his preference is clear. My aunt and uncle recently bought plots there too, so it seems that our relationship with Toms River will be a long one.

As cemeteries go, Toms River Jewish is appealing. It is small, so all the plots can be seen and easily reached from the roadside entrance. The cemetery is spacious and uncongested, allowing each plot more than sufficient space. It is luscious, surrounded by trees and has a peaceful appearance, the ultimate compliment for an eternal resting place.

I don't know if the physical appearance of the cemetery has any effect upon the deceased, since I assume that the soul is solely concerned with spiritual matters, but it can have an enormous effect on the family. It is comforting to know that your loved one is resting in a peaceful, well-kept setting. The right setting can also make it easier to connect with the spirit and memory of your loved one.

The first dedicated burial plot mentioned in the bible is the cave in Hebron that Abraham purchased after his wife Sarah's death. All of the patriarchs and matriarchs were subsequently buried there. The only exception is Rachel, who is buried in Bethlehem, where she died. Today, the Cave of the Patriarchs and Rachel's Tomb are places of pilgrimage and prayer, where supplicants ask their saintly ancestors to intercede with the Almighty on their behalf.

Visiting the graves of holy people to ask for their assistance is an ancient custom that is widely practiced today. Many small towns and villages in Eastern Europe lucky enough to have famous rabbis buried in their ancient Jewish cemeteries are the beneficiaries of Jewish pilgrims who make the journey to pray at the graves. One of the most pronounced examples of this is the grave of the Chasidic master Rabbi Nachman of Breslov, in the Ukrainian town of Uman.

Rabbi Nachman, grandson of the Ba'al Shem Tov (founder of the Hasidic movement), was recognized and accepted as a holy man and miracle worker. Rabbi Nachman declared, "When my days are ended and I leave this world, I will intercede for anyone who comes to my grave, recites the Ten Psalms of the General Remedy, and gives some charity. No matter how serious his sins and transgressions, I will do everything in my power to save him and cleanse him. I will span the length and breadth of the Creation for him. By his sidelocks I will pull him out of Hell!" He also said, "Anyone who has the privilege of being with the *Rebbe* on Rosh HaShanah is entitled to be very, very happy". Since his passing, in 1810, followers have journeyed to Uman on Rosh Hashanah to pray at his grave. Today, over 25,000 men from all across the Jewish world visit his grave on Rosh Hashanah. The local Ukrainian business people are most anxiously praying for this pilgrimage to continue.

Judaism considers burial in the earth the best way of honoring both the body and the soul of the deceased, based on the verse in the Book of Genesis, "For you are dust, and to dust you shall return." Cremation and out of the ground burial are prohibited. The human body must be buried whole with all of its components, including its blood, when physically possible. Jewish law demands that great effort be expended to assure that this is done. Tampering with, dismembering, or damaging the body in any way is considered severely insulting and painful to the soul. Autopsies and organ donation are forbidden, other than for life saving purposes.

One of the foundations of Jewish theology is the belief in the resurrection of the dead. When the Almighty wills it, the bodies of the righteous will be resurrected and reunited with their souls. Jews recite a blessing three times a day that declares, "Blessed are You our God who resurrects the dead". The following prayer, recited each morning, also speaks of the restoration of souls to dead bodies:

My G-d, the soul that You have placed into me is pure.

You created it; You formed it; You breathed it into me;

*And You preserve it within me. You will eventually
take it from me, and restore it within me in Time to Come.*

As long as the soul is within me, I give thanks before you,

Lord my G-d and G-d of my fathers, Master of all works,

*Lord of all souls. Blessed are You, G-d, Who restores souls
to dead bodies.*

According to the prophecy of Ezekiel, the bodies of the righteous will be moved to the Land of Israel before their resurrection. Based on this prophecy, Jews throughout history have gone to extraordinary lengths to be buried in Israel. This is also the basis of the custom to sprinkle earth from the holy land over the deceased before sealing the casket. A proper Jewish burial is considered a prerequisite for resurrection. The exception is when proper burial was denied by outside forces. The martyrs murdered in the holocaust and throughout Jewish history who were never properly buried will, without question, be resurrected.

We escorted the casket to the grave where Mom would be laid to rest. The rabbi said some appropriate words of eulogy. Since it was after noon on Friday, when prayers relating to mourning are omitted in deference to the approaching Sabbath, the traditional graveside prayer of *Tziduk Hadin - Righteous Judgement*, was not recited. The prayer, which is a poem, accepts God's judgment and trusts in His salvation.

> The Rock, His work is perfect, for all His ways are justice; a G-d of faithfulness and without iniquity, righteous and just is He.

> The Rock, perfect in all His works. Who can say to Him 'What have You done?' He rules below and above, He brings death and restores life, brings down to the grave and raises up from there.

> The Rock, perfect in all His deeds. Who can say to Him, 'What do You do?' You Who says and fulfills, do undeserved kindness with us, and in the merit of him [Isaac] who was bound [on the altar] like a lamb, hearken and grant our request.

Righteous One in all His ways, O Rock Who is perfect, slow to anger and abundant in mercy, take pity and spare both parents and children, for to You, O Lord, pertain forgiveness and mercy.

Righteous are You, Lord, to bring death and to restore life, for in Your hands are entrusted all spirits. Far be it from You to erase our memory. Look towards us with mercy, for Yours, O Lord, are mercy and forgiveness.

A man, whether he be a year old, or whether he lives a thousand years, what does it profit him? For is it not as if he has never been? Blessed be the True Judge, Who brings death and restores life.

Blessed be He, for His judgment is true, as He scans everything with His eye, and He rewards man according to his account and his judgment. Let all give praise to His Name.

We know, Lord, that Your judgment is right. You are righteous when You speak and pure when You judge, and none shall question Your judgments. Righteous are You, Lord, and Your judgments are just.

You are the True Judge, Who judges with righteousness and truth. Blessed is the True Judge, for all of His judgments are righteous and true.

The soul of every living creature is in Your hand, righteousness fills Your right and left hand. Have mercy on the remnant of the flock under Your hand, and say to the angel of death, 'Hold back your hand!'

You are great in counsel and mighty in action, Your eyes are watching all the ways of man, to give man according to his ways and according to the fruit of his deeds.

That is to say that the Lord is Just; He is my Strength, and there is no injustice in Him.

The Lord has given and the Lord has taken. May the Name of the Lord be blessed.

He, being compassionate, pardons iniquity, and does not destroy; time and again He turns away His anger, and does not arouse all His wrath.

I watched as relatives and friends carefully lowered the casket into the grave. Even after her passing I had still been able to at least be physically close to her. Now Mom was leaving forever. My heart sank along with her casket. My tears flowed faster, racing to emerge while there was still the chance of glimpsing the last physical manifestation of the woman who gave me life, and who lived for me. Oh, how it hurt. There is no way for me to describe the pain in words. Those who have stood in my place understand. Those who haven't will hopefully not, for a long time. But eventually they will.

The casket lay in the grave. Now it was time to cover it with earth. It is a sign of honor and respect to physically bury the deceased at the funeral. The custom is for people to take turns filling in the grave. The shovel is not passed from one person to the next. It is left in the ground for the next person to take, to signify that death should not be contagious.

The mourners are meant to throw the first clump of earth into the grave. The thought of throwing earth on the Mom's casket was terrifying and excruciatingly painful. Watching Mom's burial was nearly unbearable for me. Now tradition mandated that I participate with my own hands. I stepped forward and picked up the shovel. Using the back of the shovel, to show my reluctance, I pushed a clump of earth into the grave. I heard the thump of the earth hitting the casket. I put the shovel down and sadly walked away to watch the rest of the burial.

It was important for me to physically participate in the burial for it provided me with a level of closure I could not have otherwise achieved. Helping to bury Mom forced my mind and my heart to accept her death as final. Without doing so, my healing process could not begin.

One by one people took the shovel and, lovingly and respectfully, filled in the grave. I could see from their faces and from their actions that they were pouring out their love along with the earth. They diligently worked until the grave was completely filled and a mound of earth several inches high covered it. There was a palpable sense of closure.

The last part of the burial service was the recitation of the *Kaddish,* a prayer which I will explain in depth later in this book. My father and I stood in front of Mom's grave and recited the ancient words in unison. My sobs forced me to stop several times during the prayer.

Chanting the *Kaddish* was emotionally wrenching for me. It signified the end of an intense struggle for life and the beginning of a yearlong period of mourning.

CHAPTER 6

EXPRESSION AND ACCEPTANCE

I've often wondered why music is prohibited at Jewish funerals and throughout the entire mourning period. As a musician, I find this particularly vexing. Music touches the soul and can bring it to soaring heights or abysmal lows. Why not use it to create or reinforce an air of sadness?

Perhaps the effect music has on the mind and soul is too powerful. Jewish tradition might have feared that music would bring Man to depths of despair and depression from which he would be unable to extract himself. I once saw a Hungarian film (Bloody Sunday) in which scores of individuals are driven to suicide while listening to a melancholy song titled "Bloody Sunday". Judaism wants mourners to grieve, but never to despair or become depressed. Mournful music at a funeral would be too intense and overpowering.

Another reason for the absence of music in Jewish mourning rites might reflect Judaism's preference for organic experiences. The mourner's sadness and grief should come from within, not as a result of an artificial stimulant such as music or, for that matter, drugs. The mourner might rely on the sorrowful atmosphere created by music instead of expressing his true feelings of pain and loss, which is a vital part of the healing process.

The sages who established the Jewish mourning customs understood the grieving process. Every law, custom, and tradition was created to help mourners properly and fully express their emotions so that they can then begin the process of healing. The first, and possibly most important, part of the mourning process is acceptance. The Jewish funeral and burial is structured to help mourners reach a level of acceptance. Without acceptance, there can be no healing. Mom's funeral forced me to accept her passing, and allowed me to mourn and begin to heal.

Shortly after her passing, I posted the following note on my Facebook page:

> My Mom, Yehudit Bat Elimelech, left this world on Erev Shabbat, the 18th of Tamuz (July 10th). In the merit of the prayers and mitzvot of hundreds of Jews, she was blessed with a few extra days of strength to spend with her family.
>
> She told us that she wasn't afraid of death, and that she loved us dearly, that we were the reason for her very existence. She was at peace with the knowledge that I would be well cared for by my wife, whom she loved like her own daughter, and that we would be there to care for her beloved husband of forty eight years, my father. We told her that we loved her so

dearly, and we thanked her for giving us everything that was in her power to give. We told her not to worry about us. On her last night in this world, we prayed with her, said the Shema, blessed her and said good bye. A few hours later she was gone.

I feel deeply sad that my Mom can no longer share her love with us, and frustrated that her life was cut short just as she was beginning to enjoy her new family and look forward to a new generation, but I take some consolation knowing that we were there to escort her to the next world with love, and that she was at peace with her life and legacy. May our prayers, good deeds, and Torah study elevate her soul and bring her eternal peace and comfort.

As for me...I will never forget you, Mom. Your spirit will live on in my heart and the hearts of your future generations. I know you will always look out for us and protect us, as you did your entire life. I miss you very much. Goodbye Mom.

CHAPTER 7

SHIVA

Judaism prescribes four distinct stages of mourning. The first is *Aninut*, discussed previously, which begins at the moment of death and concludes with the burial. The second stage, called *Shiva*, begins after burial and lasts for seven days. The third stage, called *Shloshim*, lasts for thirty days and includes the *Shiva*. The final stage lasts for twelve months, beginning with the burial, and only applies to a son or daughter mourning for a parent. The laws and customs of each mourning period will be discussed as it occurs chronologically.

The *Shiva*, which is Hebrew for seven, is observed in the home of one of the mourners. Dad and I chose to observe *Shiva* in my aunt's house in Morris Plains, NJ, close to where many of our relatives live, where we could mourn without worrying about the everyday necessities of life.

During *Shiva* mourners wear the same garment torn at the funeral, sit on the floor or on low stools, and do not wear shoes. They are prohibited from taking haircuts and shaving, bathing for pleasure, and engaging in any form of entertainment, including the study of Torah. Mirrors in the *Shiva* house are covered to remind the mourner, and possibly the visitors, not to be overly concerned with physical appearance, for it is the soul, not the body, that lives on in eternity. Mourners should not leave the house for the entire seven day period. A *minyan*, comprised of at least ten Jewish men over the age of thirteen, is organized in the house to allow the mourner the opportunity to recite the *Kaddish*, which can only be recited with a *minyan*, at each of the three daily prayer services. A husband is obligated to recite the *Kaddish* for thirty days. A son must say *Kaddish* for eleven months.

Shiva is both a private and a public display of mourning. Since public displays of mourning are prohibited on the Sabbath, the mourner must leave the house to attend synagogue on the Sabbath in order to recite *Kaddish*. He must also wear shoes and good clothing, and sit on a chair. At the conclusion of the Sabbath, the *Shiva* restrictions return.

Since my aunt's house is not in walking distance to a synagogue and driving is prohibited on the Sabbath, I needed to find a place to spend that first Sabbath of my *Shiva* where I could walk to synagogue to recite *Kaddish*. Natalie and I decided to stay on the Upper West Side of Manhattan, at the home of our close friends Jerry and Marci Litwin, where I knew I would feel comfortable enough to not be sociable.

I lived on the Upper West Side for almost fifteen years before moving to Israel, and was an active and visible member of the vibrant Jewish community there. I had not been back to the neighborhood for many months and most people were unaware of Mom's passing, so I knew that people would be anxious to greet me and "shmooze". This was the last thing I wanted to do. I had just buried my mother. I was not capable of smiling. I didn't want to. All I wanted was to grieve.

The synagogue I planned to attend that Friday night would be packed with several hundred worshipers. It would be impossible to remain unnoticed. On the walk there we passed a guy who I had not seen for a couple of years. He greeted me warmly. I couldn't ignore him, but I also couldn't bring myself to appear happy. I'm not great at hiding my feelings. I managed a weak smile and apologized for not being able to stop and chat. I needed to get to synagogue in time to say *Kaddish*. Moments later we ran into someone else. He asked, "What's new?" I gave up. No more games. "Actually, my mom just died and I need to rush to synagogue." I didn't need to say another word. It was quite a conversation stopper, like a slap in the face, but it was the truth, the only thing on my mind, so it would have to do.

A mourner, if capable, is obligated to lead the service as cantor, so I informed the rabbi that I was in *Shiva*, and led the afternoon service. The prayers that are recited to welcome the Sabbath are joyous ones, and mourners in *Shiva* are prohibited from participating in them. I left the sanctuary and waited in the lobby until after the initial prayers. Then an announcement was made that there was a mourner entering the synagogue, and I was escorted into the sanctuary as the congregation recited the traditional phrase of consolation:

Hamakom yenachem etchem b'toch shar aveyley tzion v'yerushalayim

May the Place comfort you among the mourners of Zion and Jerusalem

All eyes were on me. I hated the attention, but at least everyone knew now, so I wouldn't have to fake being happy anymore.

That Sabbath was extremely hard on me. I was forced to go public when I could only handle staying private, in my own space, with my memories and sorrow. It was too soon. It would have been different if I had already observed even a couple of *Shiva* days. The pain would have been a tiny bit less raw, the wound slightly less opened.

We drove back to my parents', or I guess I should say my dad's, house on Saturday night and arrived at my aunt's home early Sunday morning, ready to stay for the remainder of the *Shiva*.

CHAPTER 8

ETIQUETTE

Visiting a mourner during *Shiva* is considered one of the greatest acts of kindness. It can bring tremendous comfort to the mourners, help them deal with the pain and sorrow of their loss and begin the slow healing process. Jewish custom dictates specific rules of etiquette for visitors to follow in a *Shiva* house, designed to help them assist, rather than disrupt, the mourner at this important stage in the mourning process.

Here are some of the rules:

Do not initiate conversation with the mourner.

The mourner must initiate. This gives the mourner the option to remain silent, if that is what he feels he needs to do. Most people find it extremely difficult to simply sit silently in the presence of other people so they will say something to relieve that discomfort. They forget that their purpose at the *Shiva* is not to make themselves feel comfortable, but to comfort the mourner. If the mourner is comforted by silence, then that is what the visitor must offer. This means that there can be a room full of visitors sitting in silence. It is powerful, and heartbreaking. I tried to say something, even a single word, just to enable a visitor to speak.

Many times I would have preferred to remain silent, but I didn't want to make anyone feel awkward. I also realized that most visitors were ignorant of the rules and would speak first anyway, so I tried to beat them to it and save them from breaking the rule.

Do not try to take the mourner's mind off mourning with stories, jokes, or matters unrelated to mourning.

The purpose of the *Shiva* is to give the mourner the opportunity to experience his sadness and share memories with friends and loved ones. This is a vital part of the grieving, and healing, process. Distracting the mourner robs him of this opportunity and makes the healing process more difficult. I actually found it insulting, for both me and Mom, when visitors tried to lighten the mood by talking about things unrelated to my mourning. I realize they had only the best intentions, but that still didn't make up for their insensitivity. Weren't they aware of the pain that I was experiencing? Didn't they understand that distracting me would only delay my healing?

I think visitors try to lighten and distract because they either are unable to handle the somber and mournful mood around them, or they sincerely want to help, and see this as their only practical way of doing so. My message to visitors is that it's normal and therapeutic to mourn and be sad. Just being there for the mourner is a great comfort. No words are necessary, but if you must speak, let the words and actions of the mourner guide your conversation.

Do not engage in unrelated side conversations with other visitors.

The only valid reason for you to visit during *Shiva* is to comfort the mourner and to show respect for the deceased. Doing anything else is disrespectful and just plain insensitive. If you need to catch up with someone you haven't seen or spoken to in a long time, do it outside or at least in another room where the mourner will not hear your joyful reunion. It's usually wonderful to hear family members laughing and getting along. Not at a *Shiva*. It sounds so intuitive that I feel out of line even writing about this, but I've experienced it and seen it happen so many times that I feel I must pound this point home. Stay focused on the mourner. Period.

Don't ask the mourner how he's doing.

He's probably experiencing tremendous grief, pain, possibly guilt, confusion, and helplessness. Instead, ask or offer to help him with anything he might need in his time of sorrow. Every time someone asked me how I was doing, I felt torn. I wanted to answer the question honestly and tell the questioner exactly how I was feeling and what I was experiencing, but I knew that they really didn't want all that information and they probably couldn't handle hearing it. I couldn't be polite and lie and say things were ok. That just isn't me. You ask me a question, you deserve a real answer. I usually sighed and said something like, "it's not easy" or "what can I say?"

Do ask the mourner to tell you about his deceased love one.

Speaking about them is therapeutic. Your interest also shows honor and respect for the deceased. If the mourner is reluctant to speak, don't press them.

Most visitors asked about how Mom died, a perfectly legitimate question. I appreciated the opportunity to tell the story of Mom's last days, how she accepted her destiny, and how she left the world in peace. I told the story of how the *Shabbat* light burned out the night before her death. The first time I spoke about her death I could barely get through it without crying. The more I talked about it the easier it became. It was still incredibly painful, but the shock was no longer there.

CHAPTER 9

BAGELS

I expected my relatives to pay a *Shiva* visit, and they did. I was impressed that many of my friends and former students and congregants made the journey from Manhattan. Even though it was only about a fifty minute car ride, most Manhattanites don't have cars, so getting to NJ was a chore. Above all, I was deeply touched by the visitors who had been customers at Mom's store. Their presence was a real tribute to the kind of person Mom was.

In 1982 Mom decided to open a bagel shop in Springfield, NJ. Ever since I was a kid I remember Mom buying bagels from a small shop in Elizabeth, our then home town. They were the best bagels around and we loved them. We were hit hard by the recessions of the mid seventies and early eighties, and Mom went back to work to help make ends meet, working as a salesperson at several large clothing store chains. She understood that the way to financial independence was through business ownership, and she loved those bagels, so she scraped money together from our meager savings and got busy.

Mom was a great businesswoman and a fantastic cook, but she wasn't a bagel maker. No problem. Over the years, Mom had gotten friendly with Manny, the Portuguese bagel maker at the small bagel shop we patronized. Perhaps this was part of her strategy all along. I think, at least initially, she was just being her usual friendly self. Mom formed a partnership with Manny. She would run the business end and be out front with the customers, and he would do what he did best: make great bagels.

Mom, with Dad's constant help, dived into her new endeavor. She picked Springfield because it was an affluent town with a large Jewish community (it's true, Jews eat more bagels than the average American!). It was also far enough from Elizabeth to avoid competing with the Elizabeth shop, which just happened to be owned by a shady, gangster-like character (whose name I will omit for obvious reasons). I guess it wasn't far enough. Mom and Dad put everything they had into getting that store ready. The night before the grand opening, the store was fire bombed and severely damaged. Coincidence?

Most people would have thrown in the towel at that point. Mom was not most people. She had a temper that you did not want to be on the receiving end of. She probably inherited it from her father, the tough officer. The unfortunate "explosive coincidence" simply made her more determined to succeed, if only to show that NOBODY could push Jeane Singer around. Luckily my parents had insured the store. A few months later, Bagel Supreme opened on Mountain Avenue in Springfield, NJ. It was a smashing success.

After a few years Mom decided to split with Manny. She needed the freedom to run her business the way she saw fit, without anyone interfering, so she sold Manny her share and started working on a new location. By this time Mom knew just about everything there was to know about the bagel business.

The traditional bagel making process has several stages. First you need to make the dough. You throw very specific measures of water, salt, flour, yeast, and malt into a dough mixer and hit the "on" button. After the dough is mixed, which could take anywhere from ten to twenty minutes depending on the quantity of dough and temperature, you place the dough on a table, cut a strip of dough, and roll it. You then twist a piece around your hand, detach it from the strip, and press down with your palm to connect the ends, forming a small ring of rolled dough: a bagel.

After you form your bagels and arrange them on rectangular wooden boards that can each hold over three dozen, you let the bagels rise. The right amount of rising time is very subjective, depending on how you want your bagels to look and feel. Too long and you'll be selling oversized balloons. Too short and you'll be serving jawbreakers. Since heat accelerates the rising process, the bagels are usually placed in a cooler, to better control the process. Once the dough is ready, the bagels are ready for baking.

The bagels are first dunked in a kettle of boiling water, for anywhere from a few seconds to a minute, to give them their shiny crust. Then they are placed face down on narrow wooden boards, sprinkled with toppings, and placed into a 500 degree oven with rotating shelves. After a couple of rounds in the oven, the boards are flipped over, placing the bagels face up. The bagels are then baked until ready. How they end up depends on many factors including the type of oven, water, degree of heat, and length of baking time. It's a pretty complex and exacting process, and Mom mastered it.

The only thing Mom couldn't do on her own was actually form, or roll, the dough into the bagel shape, which is a lot harder than it sounds, especially if you're rolling hundreds at a time. There were bagel machines that could do the forming, but Mom wouldn't hear of it. She insisted that handmade bagels were better, and she would only manufacture and sell the best. Manny wasn't the only bagel maker around. With the help of some of her suppliers, Mom tracked down a tattooed, smoking, foul mouthed, slightly deranged Jewish biker from Brooklyn who was a bagel making savant. He was quite a character but he rolled great bagels, and Mom kept him in line with her demanding, yet endearing, personality.

Soon after selling her Springfield store, Mom opened Super Duper Bagels in Livingston, NJ, an affluent suburban town with a large and growing Jewish population. Super Duper was located in a small strip of stores off a main road. It was tiny, not visible from the main road, and there was already a popular, well established bagel shop less than half a mile away. It had all the ingredients for failure, except for two things: the product and Mom.

The bagels Mom made at Super Duper were actually "super duper". I'm still not exactly sure what made them that way. Dad and I subsequently opened other bagel stores and we used the same recipe and technique, but somehow, our bagels never were as good as Mom's. Maybe the Livingston water was different, or perhaps it was the small size of her oven, but I think the real reason for the difference was Mom. She put her heart and soul into making sure that each bagel came out perfect. It wasn't just a business for her. Like a master chef in a five star restaurant, Mom took enormous pride in her work, and would settle for nothing less than perfection. When she saw a bagel that didn't meet her standards, she quickly put it aside and made sure that her bakers corrected whatever it was that caused them to create the faulty product. She was a demanding boss, but made sure to praise and reward her employees when warranted.

It wasn't only the bagels that were super duper. Mom sold cheese and fish spreads, made bagel sandwiches, and sliced Nova Scotia smoked salmon thinner than paper. She would slice so much salmon that her arm would actually go numb. It was the same fish that everyone else sold but, when Mom sliced it, it tasted better. It was like that with everything in the store. There were literally lines out the door, especially on Sunday mornings.

People came from all over to buy Mom's super duper bagels. Visitors would take them on airplanes to far off places. Students would take them back to their colleges. The store is still there, but the bagels are just not quite the same. It's something I can't really describe. If you tasted them, you know what I mean. If you didn't get the chance, you'll have to live with the knowledge that you missed out on the best tasting bagel ever made.

Bagels and lox were only part of what made Super Duper so successful. The other part was Mom. People came there just to see her. Why? Mom was an old school store owner. Her store was her home and when you came to her home you had to mind your manners and play by her rules. She was in charge, and you were her guest. As long as you respected that relationship, you were her best friend and she bent over backwards to make sure you got the best of everything. If you ignored that relationship and disrespected her by questioning how she ran her "home", she would have no qualms about telling you to be someone else's guest instead.

One sure way of "dissing" Mom was to ask if the bagels were fresh. The bagels were always fresh. The store was so busy that they never got the chance to sit out for too long. Under no circumstances were they ever from a previous day. Just imagine asking a temperamental French master chef if the dish he just cooked especially for you was fresh. Well, asking Mom that question was just as bad. If you were lucky and she was in a good mood, she would just get really annoyed and respond with an exasperated, "yes, EVERYTHING is fresh". You'd get your fresh bagels, but no banter. If you were clueless enough to ask that question on a Sunday morning when the place was a madhouse with nonstop lines out the door, you might get, "if you don't think they're fresh, you don't need to buy them!" I think one or two people might have been insulted and left. The rest relished the excitement, prayed for the opportunity to see someone put in their place, and learned how to behave. I always told Mom not to take the customer comments personally. So what if they ask if it's fresh? Just let it go. But she couldn't. It was a direct attack on her integrity, and she had to strike back. Mom didn't take crap from anyone.

Most regular customers were nice to Mom, and she treated them like family. She knew their names, what they did, and how old their kids were. She listened to their stories and problems, and with a select few, even shared some of her own. Interacting with Jeane was part of what made coming to Super Duper Bagels special.

Super Duper was strictly kosher under rabbinical supervision and closed on the Sabbath and Jewish holidays. Mom was proud of her kosher status and that observant Jews, including her own son, could eat her products without worry. It didn't hurt business either, since her's was the only kosher bagel shop in the area. Mom made friends with the supervising rabbis, and they trusted her completely. She would allow no uncertified product to ever enter her store or her home.

Any leftover bagels at the end of the day would be donated to one of several charities that came by to pick them up. Her favorite was the Chabad run Rabbinical College in Morristown, NJ. A Jewish mother, she made sure the *yeshiva* boys got some spreads and salads, not just a few left over bagels. They were rarely disappointed.

The busiest day of the year was unquestionably the day before the Jewish holiday of *Yom Kippur. Yom Kippur* is a fast day that begins in the evening and lasts for slightly over 24 hours. Traditionally, Jews break their fast on bagels, lox, and all the other goodies that you're probably imagining now. Since business is prohibited on the holiday, all the food needs to be purchased before it begins. Mom would begin taking orders a week before the holiday. There were only so many bagels that she could physically produce in a day. If you waited until the last minute you were sure to miss your chance at breaking your fast on a Super Duper bagel.

Mom and her staff worked throughout the night to prepare all the orders. She sliced dozens of Nova Scotia smoked salmons, thousands of slices, until her hand simply went dumb. The lines of customers did not end until every last bagel and slice of lox were sold. At around noon time Mom closed the store, exhausted. She was usually too wiped to go to evening services, but she made sure that her customers would be well fed the next evening.

An old Yiddish saying declares, "Man plans, and God laughs." Yet, we continue to plan for our future, and strive to control it. We work hard and save money today so that we don't have to worry in our later years. While this is obviously the prudent path to take, it shouldn't make us overlook the reality of life; that we have no control. How many stories have you heard of people who saved their pennies only to be stricken with a terminal illness before having the chance to enjoy the fruits of their labor? Man plans, and God laughs. We have no choice but to plan for the future and to hope for the best.

Mom owned Super Duper Bagels for close to twenty five years. I don't think she ever missed a day of work, even when she was undergoing chemotherapy treatments. She didn't want people to know she was sick. She was too proud to receive their sympathy or pitying looks. Almost a year before my wedding, Mom sold the store. It was right before the financial crisis of 2008, a good time to sell. It was a great business, but she had had enough. She realized that making money was only a means to an end.

Now that she was sufficiently comfortable financially, she wanted to relax and enjoy her golden years. No more waking up at 4:00am to "make the bagels". She looked forward to traveling and eventually enjoying grandchildren. God had different plans.

CHAPTER 10

TRANSITION

Observing *Shiva* gave me the opportunity to reflect on Mom's life and death without worrying about work, food, appearance, or sociability. It allowed me to share my thoughts and feelings with people that cared about Mom and me, and it gave them a chance to show their love and respect for us. During those seven days of reflection and semi-isolation, I was able to transition from shock at Mom's passing to accepting that she was gone forever. My deep sadness and pain were still real, but I could now begin to integrate them into my everyday life without being immobilized by them.

I don't know how someone who has just lost a loved one can go from the burial directly into regular daily life. Most people do just that. They're back at work, taking care of business, going to meetings, doing lunch, running errands, getting back into their normal routines as quickly as possible. I guess they think that the best way to deal with their grief is to ignore it and move on. The problem with this is that it doesn't work. Their grief is still very much with them, but they've shoved it into a drawer and locked away, so it seems as though they've successfully dealt with it.

I once counseled a congregant who was having difficulty meeting the right man. It turns out that she was meeting good men, but she wasn't willing to commit because she feared it would prevent her from doing what she felt she needed to do. When I asked what was it that she needed to accomplish, she didn't know. We discussed some more and she told me that her mother had died several years before and she never observed *Shiva* for her. She never properly mourned, and so, she never properly healed. The wound was still open, and it hurt. She needed to experience the equivalent of a *Shiva*, to mourn her mother, and heal her wound, in order to feel complete enough to commit to another person.

That woman carried her pain and guilt for several years. Many people carry their pain and guilt for much longer. It affects the way they treat spouses, children, and most of all, themselves. Pain and grief over the loss of a loved one must be expressed as fully as possible in order for the mourner to be able to move forward in a healthy way. *Shiva* is a perfect way of doing this. Other types of serious mourning and reflection can also do the job. However you choose to do it, give yourself the time and space to begin to heal. A day or two is not enough.

There's nothing abnormal or "unmanly" about taking time to grieve. Don't get caught in the macho trap of thinking that a strong man (or woman) should bear the pain while maintaining appearances and carrying on as if nothing happened. Something did happen, something life changing, that can't be ignored, brushed aside, or buried in the trash bin of insignificant events.

The grief from losing a loved one exempts no one. Denying it can leave lifelong scars.

Observing *Shiva* is not easy. In an age when information travels in milliseconds, seven days can feel like an eternity. Towards the end of the week you may feel like you've had enough, and are ready to rejoin the outside world and get back to your normal routine. I think doing so is a mistake. There is value in using the entire seven day period to mourn and grieve. Otherwise, the Jewish sages would not have made it last for that period. Trust their wisdom.

Shiva is not only for the mourner; it is for the entire community. The community plays an indispensable role in the mourner's grieving and healing process. This idea stretches back to biblical times. According to the bible, coming into contact with death, by actually touching or by being under the same roof as a corpse or by entering a graveyard, makes an individual ritually impure. The only way to become pure again is to have the ashes of a *"perfectly red cow that has no blemish and has never had a yoke placed upon it. (Numbers 19:2)"* sprinkled on him by a *Kohen*, a Jewish priest. After sprinkling the ashes, the *Kohen* who did the sprinkling is now considered impure and must immerse in a *Mikvah*, a ritual pool of water, to purify. Sounds illogical. The one who purifies becomes impure? Also, in all other cases of ritual impurity, immersing in a *Mikvah* provides sufficient purification. Why does death related impurity require the ash sprinkling? Rabbi J.B. Soloveitchik explains that the very concept of death shakes Man to his core, stripping him of any sense of control over his own destiny and leaving him shocked and depressed. Death wounds him so severely that he cannot heal himself. He must turn to someone else for help to cope with his grief and emerge from the precipice of despair. The person offering help cannot escape unscathed from his interaction with one who was so close to death. He too leaves shaken, but in a much less drastic way, so that he can purify himself in the *Mikvah*. The visitors to the *Shiva* house expose themselves to pain and sorrow to save the mourner from drowning in a wave of despair and depression.

It's important for a mourner to have someone to sprinkle the ashes on him, someone to confide in, to discuss his feelings with, and express his sadness, without shame or fear. The *Shiva* tries to fill that need.

CHAPTER 11

QUESTIONS

I often felt like asking the obvious question of God: why? Why did God have to take Mom at a time when she had so much to live for? I felt like asking, but I didn't. How could I when so many die young? Everyone knows of someone in their twenties or thirties who was stricken with cancer or who suddenly died of a massive heart attack or aneurism. A friend of mine from college, a rabbi, in good health, died alone in his apartment at age 32. A fellow in my building, in his late thirties, was found dead in his apartment after having returned from his usual jogging workout. A father of two in his mid thirties that I know was diagnosed with leukemia and died two years later, after putting up a valiant fight. At seventy two, Mom had lived a full life. I wish with all my heart that she could have lived another year or ten or twenty, but I am grateful that she lived longer than most people on this planet.

As a man of faith, I knew the answer to my unasked question. Everyone has a mission to fulfill in their lifetime. We don't know what that exact mission is. We do know that part of that mission is to be kind and compassionate, and to help build the world that God created. We also know that once we complete our mission, we must leave this world for an eternal, spiritual, existence. Mom completed her mission. I could speculate about what that mission was. Part of it was definitely giving me life. Perhaps once she saw me married to someone who she knew would love and care for me, her mission was fulfilled. I'll never know, but if it brings me peace, I see no harm in speculating.

I've seen it happen too many times to be coincidence. A parent dies soon after their child gets engaged or married or has a child of their own. At first glance it seems cruel. Upon closer examination, it can be seen as a blessing. Not that the death of a parent is a blessing, but that it occurs when the child has the loving support to deal with it. The Talmud teaches that God always sends the cure before the malady. In my case, I found my wife nearly a year before I lost Mom. Without Natalie, my mourning experience would have been bitter and guilt ridden. I would have been angry at myself for denying Mom the joy of seeing her only son married and settled. The guilt would have worn me down. Worst of all, I would have had to deal with it all alone. I am thankful for the order in which the events transpired. The cure before the malady.

In many cases the series of events do not line up as neatly. People die tragically, suddenly, and leave behind young children, destitute families. The cure is not readily visible, but I believe it's there. It might take time, years, generations to comprehend, or we might not recognize it when it's right before our eyes, but it is there. God always sends the cure before the malady.

I still feel cheated by Mom's death, angry that she had to be taken. If I didn't feel that way, I wouldn't be a good son. Over the years I saw other people lose parents, but I couldn't imagine it happening to me. My parents would live forever. I assume this is how a soldier feels when he goes into battle. He knows people will get killed, but not him. He is invincible. I looked around me and thought, I can't believe this is happening to me. It was surreal, but it was my reality.

CHAPTER 12

KADDISH

The ritual most associated with traditional Jewish mourning is the recitation of the *Kaddish,* known as the prayer for the dead. *Kaddish,* which means holy, is a unique prayer in that it is written in Aramaic instead of the standard Hebrew. Aramaic is an ancient Semitic language that was, in ancient times, dominant in most of the Middle East. It became the everyday language of Israel during the Second Temple period (539BCE – 70CE) and within the large Babylonian Jewish community, which is probably why the *Kaddish* was composed in Aramaic. Even those who could not speak Hebrew would be able to recite *Kaddish.*

A medieval rabbinic commentary offers a mystical reason for the Aramaic text of *Kaddish.* Since *Kaddish* is such a holy and sanctified prayer, it was feared that the angels in heaven would grow jealous of the Jewish people and block their prayers from reaching the Master of the Universe. To prevent this, *Kaddish* was composed in Aramaic which, according to mystical tradition, the angels do not understand.

The text of the *Kaddish*:

Yitgadal VeYitkadash Shemay Rabah

May His great Name be exalted and sanctified

In the world that He created by His will.

May He establish His kingdom in your lifetime and in your days

And in the lifetime of the whole house of Israel,

Swiftly and soon – and say: Amen.

(The Congregation says the following line in unison:)

May His great name be blessed forever and all time.

Blessed and praised, glorified and exalted,

Raised and honored, uplifted and lauded

Be the name of the Holy One, blessed be He,

Beyond any blessing, song, praise, and consolation

Uttered in the world – and say: Amen.

May there be great peace from heaven,

And life for us and all Israel – and say: Amen.

May He who makes peace in His high places,

Make peace for us and all Israel – and say: Amen.

Now that you've read the entire *Kaddish* prayer, you're no doubt wondering why it's commonly referred to as the prayer for the dead. There is absolutely nothing in the prayer that even remotely relates to death. The *Kaddish* is basically just one long exaltation of the Almighty, and is recited several times in every prayer service by the cantor, usually at the end of each section of the service. Why, then, is the *Kaddish* associated with death?

Since Judaism believes that God's deeds and actions are completely just and righteous, including those that appear otherwise, we are obligated to praise God in bad times as in good. This is why we recite a blessing upon hearing of someone's passing. This is also why we praise God by reciting the ultimate praise, the *Kaddish,* as a response to death and as an acceptance of God's absolute justice.

Jewish mystical tradition offers another answer to explain the connection between *Kaddish* and death. Imagine that God is a general and we are all his soldiers. A successful general emerges from battle with minimal casualties. When soldiers are killed, the general's detractors claim that he is incompetent, unfit to lead. His reputation is tarnished, his fame diminished. God is not only a general who has lost a soldier, he is a parent who has lost a child. When a person dies, God's glorious name is diminished. *Kaddish* exalts His name and restores it to its previous glory. Who better to repair the damaged name than a mourner who feels the emptiness and loss caused by the death of a loved one.

This idea is also behind the traditional phrase of condolence offered to the mourner:

*Hamakom yenachem etchem b'toch shar aveyley tzion
v'yerushalayim*

*May the Place comfort you among the mourners of Zion
and Jerusalem*

The *Place* refers to God. The only other time this terminology is
used is in a prayer for those in danger or captivity. The Hebrew
word for place is also the word for space, as in "give me some
space" or "this is my space." When God's children are dying or in
danger, God appears to be missing. There is a space in the world
that seems empty. It is that representation of God's presence, the
empty space, that comforts the mourner experiencing the
vacuum left by their loved one.

The bible recounts that the people mourned the passing of
Aaron, the High Priest, for thirty days. Based on this, the
mourning period for relatives other than parents is limited to
thirty days. Why does a child mourn and say *Kaddish* for a parent
for nearly a full year? A parent's sorrow over losing a child is
much greater than a child's for a parent, yet a parent mourns and
recites *Kaddish* for only thirty days. The additional months of
Kaddish are to show the proper honor and respect due to a
parent, in fulfillment of the fifth of the Ten Commandments,
"Honor your father and mother." This obligation continues even
after the parent's passing.

I've always taken my obligation to honor and respect my
parents seriously. It wasn't always easy. Mom and I didn't always
see eye to eye. Mom was very emotional and had a temper that
could make a scorned Latin lover seem timid. I seem to have

inherited her temper. When we disagreed, the neighbors knew it. As I grew older I tried to control how I interacted with Mom, but I was rarely successful. I kept trying, and I did get better, but I never could fully control myself. Despite all the fighting and the tears, we never stopped loving each other and I never forgot that she was my mother, who gave me life and unconditional love.

Memory can be tricky. It can be authentic, selective, or fabricated, and no one other than the actual owner or conjurer of that memory will ever know the truth. Sometimes, even the owner won't. The only balances to memory are hard evidence, such as a letter or photograph, or firsthand testimony. I can tell people that I was a fat kid in third grade, but my third grade class photo will prove me wrong. I can remember my friend buying a coat at Macy's, but she can correct me by declaring that she bought it at Bloomingdales.

Without evidence or firsthand testimony, there is no way to conclusively prove or disprove a memory. Its authenticity lies exclusively with the rememberer. Most people leave behind little evidence to attest to anything other than their appearance. Their character and reputation is left entirely in the hands of the relatives and friends that survive them. The responsibility for perpetuating their memory usually rests with their children and spouse. In cases of grave parental misconduct or abuse, it may be necessary for the child to actively remember and recount their parent's deeds as part of their healing process. In most cases, children have the option to choose which memories to share and which to keep private.

I was blessed with loving parents who always put my needs before their own. I don't think an entire hour ever passed during which Mom did not think about me and my welfare. That doesn't mean that I agree with everything she did or believed in. There were things about Mom that I choose not to emulate. In the forty three years that we spent together there were times and incidents that were stressful, hurtful, embarrassing, and insulting for both of us. Time has erased most of them from my memory. Some remain with me, refusing to disappear, hard as I may try. Will I share these memories and make them part of Mom's eternal legacy? I won't, for it is my sacred duty to honor Mom. It is my final, everlasting, gift, the greatest gift a child can give a parent.

In a story cited in several ancient Jewish sources, the great sage Rabbi Akiva was walking in a graveyard and had a vision in which a renowned sinner who had died implored him to teach his young son the *Kaddish* so that he could recite it in synagogue and save his father from the torments of punishment in the afterlife. Rabbi Akiva found the boy and taught him. The man reappeared to Rabbi Akiva and blessed him. His son's recitation of *Kaddish* had released him from perdition.

Based on this source, a child can save a parent from torment in *Gehinnom* by reciting the *Kaddish*. According to Jewish theology, no person is perfect. Even Moses, the greatest prophet to have ever lived, sinned and was punished by not being allowed to enter the Promised Land. Since everyone sins, everyone must endure some degree of torment in *Gehinnom*, the Jewish version of hell, in order to become purified and move on to their eternal reward. My recitation of *Kaddish* three times a day for eleven months was more than a part of my obligation to honor Mom. It was something concrete I could do for her in appreciation for all she gave me. I had the power to help ease Mom's journey through this painful process. It was a duty that I lovingly embraced and vowed to fulfill.

Mourners for siblings, spouses, or children are obligated to recite *Kaddish* for the thirty days following burial, and on the yearly anniversary of the relative's passing. Children mourning parents are obligated to recite *Kaddish* for eleven months. According to Jewish mystical tradition, souls receive their punishment in *Gehinnom* for a maximum of twelve months. Only the worst sinners remain for the full year. A child proclaims the righteousness of his parent by reciting *Kaddish* for only eleven months.

Reciting *Kaddish* three times a day for eleven months was not easy. *Kaddish* can only be said with a *minyan*, so finding a prayer service with ten adult Jewish males became an ongoing obsession. I remember an old television show called Northern Exposure, which featured a Jewish doctor from NY, Joel Fleischman, who was sent to practice in a tiny remote Alaskan town in order to pay off his state funded medical school scholarship. In one episode, Joel wants to recite *Kaddish* for his uncle, but as the only Jew in town, he is unable to. To help their medical *boychick* out, the townspeople scour the state of Alaska in search of nine Jewish men to complete the *minyan*. This might sound exaggerated, but a similar scenario is not unrealistic. Jewish men have gone to extraordinary lengths to say *Kaddish.*

Men who only set foot in a synagogue a handful of times in their lives suddenly become fanatically regular attendants.

Not all Jewish men take their obligation seriously. In our modern, assimilated, society, many opt to send a check to one of many organizations who offer to recite *Kaddish* in their stead, but a significant number still cling to the belief that only they can save their parents from punishment in the afterlife. They wake up early, rearrange their workday, and rush out of the office to make sure they don't miss their *Kaddish.* There's even an iphone app that helps you find the closest *minyan.*

I am lucky enough to live within a few blocks of a handful of synagogues with different service times throughout the day. Getting out of bed on rainy or blisteringly cold and dark winter mornings was not easy, but manageable. Getting to synagogue for the afternoon service in the winter was more challenging. The afternoon service is usually held right before sunset, which in the winter months can be as early as 4:00pm. This can wreak havoc on a daily schedule. In areas where large numbers of Orthodox Jews live and work you can usually find a lunchtime *minyan* in an office or place of business. Outside of those areas, or on Sundays, it's not so easy. I had to plan our Sunday visits to see my Dad in New Jersey around the afternoon service with military precision, to make sure we had lunch, visiting time, dinner at a restaurant, and were on the road in time to beat the traffic back to the city. The days when sunset fell between 6:30pm and 7:30pm were particularly inconvenient.

Travel presented my biggest challenge. Getting kosher food almost anywhere in the world today is possible, thanks to

Chabad and frozen dinners. Getting a *minyan* three times daily isn't. Vacationing in exotic or out of the way destinations was crossed off of our to do list. Work travel wasn't so easy to avoid.

I occasionally have to travel for work. I made my boss aware of my *Kaddish* situation, and he tried his best to accommodate, but there were a few times where I just couldn't avoid it. Two of those trips were overnighters, one to Irvine, CA and the other to Las Vegas. Luckily, both of those locations have thriving Jewish communities, so attending *minyan* was easy. The other two locations I had to visit were Orlando and Atlanta. Both of those cities have Orthodox congregations. The problem was that I was arriving and returning the same day. In the winter months, the earliest time to pray is usually not before 6:30am. In order to arrive at my destination by mid morning I had to take early flights. I had to travel to the airport and arrive at least an hour before the flight. You do the math: *minyan* was out of the question. Getting back home in time for afternoon service was also not feasible, given the shortness of the day. In these two instances I made sure to say *Kaddish* at least once during the twenty four hour day. It wasn't ideal, but at least I did not miss a day without *Kaddish*.

The only major journey we did take was to Israel, after the *Shiva*. The flight is around twelve hours, which translates into two missed prayer services. Wrong! At the appropriate times, as if on some secret prearranged signal, Orthodox men filtered to the back of the plane and, you guessed it: airborne *minyan*! It might have annoyed the crew and some passengers seated in the back row of the plane, but for me and the other *Kaddish* sayers, it was a Godsend.

In the first few weeks after Mom's passing I couldn't stop thinking about her. As the weeks turned into months and the normal routine of life took over I found myself thinking about her less and less. There were always moments of sadness and remembering, but they were fewer. *Kaddish* forced me to think about Mom at least three times daily. It gave me the chance to feel sad and the mechanism through which to express that sadness in a positive way. When I said those Aramaic words I felt directly connected to Mom. It was our own, secret, private moment together that no one else was privy to.

One day, the rabbi of the synagogue I was saying *Kaddish* in handed me a slip of paper with a name on it, and asked if I could keep that person in mind when I said *Kaddish,* since they had no one to say *Kaddish* for them. I thought for a moment, handed back the paper, and explained that I only had room for Mom in my thoughts. My *Kaddish* was completely and totally dedicated to her. It was our private time together, my special gift to her. This might seem selfish and hard to understand to someone who hasn't lost a parent. To those who have, it makes perfect sense.

CHAPTER 13

SHLOSHIM

The stage of mourning that follows *Shiva* is called *Shloshim*, meaning thirty, and lasts for thirty days inclusive of the *Shiva*. Shaving, haircuts, wearing new clothing, and enjoying live entertainment are prohibited. For a child mourning a parent, these prohibitions apply to the entire year, although haircuts and shaving become permissible after *Shloshim*, if the mourner is reproached for his unkempt appearance.

Natalie and I returned to Israel to pack up our belongings, tie up our affairs, and say goodbye to family and friends. We would be moving to New York, to be close to Dad and fulfill the promise we made to Mom on her deathbed.

It was a difficult month for both of us, for different reasons. I was grieving almost as intensely as during my *Shiva*. Every night, as I tried to fall asleep, I felt the immense loss, the gaping hole in my life. The only person who would ever love me in the same absolute, unconditional way was gone. Even the love of a devoted spouse cannot compare to a mother's love for her child. I tried hard not to, but I cried. I cried before bed. I cried during the day. I felt like crying most of the time in between.

161

It was a difficult time for Natalie because, besides supporting me in my time of sorrow, she had to say goodbye to her family, with whom she was extremely close, and the friends that she had made during her thirteen years in Israel. I can only imagine how hard it was for her, and I am forever grateful for her sacrifice. I had left my family a year before to be with her. Now she was leaving her's to be with me. That's what marriage is all about.

On the final day of the *Shloshim* I organized a small gathering of family and friends and delivered a talk in Mom's memory. The tradition is to study and complete a section of the Torah, usually *Mishnah*, in the merit of the deceased soul. The letters comprising the Hebrew word *Mishnah*, when rearranged, spell the word for soul, *Neshama*. Like the recitation of *Kaddish,* Torah study is a way for children to honor their parents. It also is a way to provide them with extra merits to ease their existence in the afterlife. Any performance of good deeds or commandments benefits the parent's soul, but Torah study, *Kaddish,* and charity are singled out as particularly effective.

At the *Shloshim*, instead of delivering a lecture on a section of Mishnah that I had completed, I spoke about many of the topics and experiences that are in this book. I felt it was important for people to hear my story so that they could learn from it and apply the lessons within it, if the unfortunate need should arise. It was the first time I publicly expressed my feelings about Mom's passing. I was determined not to cry. I wanted the evening to be uplifting, a tribute to Mom, not a sorrowful reliving of her death. I had to pause a few times during my talk to compose myself when tears welled up, but I kept them from dropping, and succeeded in honoring Mom, inspiring my audience, and ever so slightly lifting the pall of grief that covered my heart.

Soon after *Shloshim* I posted this note on my Facebook page:

Last week marked the end of the Shloshim, the thirty day period of mourning, for Mom. I can now shave and get my hair cut, if I'm told that my appearance warrants it, which I have been, and it does. I've also been told that my sadness should be diminished, and that my tears should no longer spontaneously flow. Everyone around me seems to accept that my mourning has ended, and that I can now once again resume my normal life, with, of course, the memory of Mom tucked neatly within my mind, to be called upon at nostalgic moments and yearly memorials. I must not be experiencing my mourning process properly.

My sadness is still great. My tears still flow, unless I hold them back, as I often do now, so as not to upset those around me, and myself. True, the intensity of the Shiva has diminished, but the wound is still open, the pain still acute. I can't ignore the fact that Mom is gone, forever. A month ago she was here, with me, full of hope and dreams, ready to share in the joys of life with husband, children, and perhaps, finally, the grandchildren that she so yearned for. Now she is gone.

It hurts, still, even after thirty days. A song, a place, a figure of speech, a photo, a wedding video, can reawaken the pain. The Kaddish that I recite three times a day prevents me from forgetting, or rather, assures that I will remember, that I have lost Mom, the one person whose love was unconditional, instinctive, and eternal. I don't think the sadness will ever go away. Perhaps it will be more manageable with time. Maybe after the year of Kaddish. Maybe never.

During our month in Israel Natalie and I sold our furniture, settled up with our landlord, and left our first home together in Tel Aviv. A few days before we left for America Natalie told me the news: she was pregnant.

CHAPTER 14

BITTERSWEET

I've never really understood the flavor known as bittersweet. How can two mortal enemies representing extreme opposites harmoniously coexist? Yet, I cannot find a better term to describe the remainder of my year of mourning: bittersweet.

I vividly remember the day Natalie told me we were going to have a baby. We were staying at her brother's house for a few days before leaving for America. I so wanted to jump up and shout for joy, but instead a floodgate of tears burst open. I wept tears of sadness and tears of joy. It was one of the happiest days of my life, and one of the saddest. I would finally be a father, but Mom would never be a grandmother. So sweet, yet so bitter.

Natalie and I rented an apartment, with magnificent views of the Hudson River, on the Upper West Side of Manhattan, my old stomping ground. All I could think of was how Mom would have approved. She would have loved looking out at the river and recalling how she looked out over that same river fifty years earlier from her and Dad's first apartment in Riverdale. This made me cry.

We went furniture shopping with Dad, and I thought of how Mom would have taken such pleasure in buying us only the best pieces, according to her impeccable taste, of course. Yes, we would have had the final say, but Mom had a way of influencing people's decisions. "You really like that?" "No, this isn't nice, you don't want that, right?" At the end she would get us whatever we wanted. It would have made her so happy. This too made me cry.

We set up house, bought new kitchenware, new linens, new everything. Mom would have wanted Natalie to have the best stuff. She would have been proud to visit. We invited Dad for Friday night *Shabbat* dinner. We went out to restaurants for dinner with him. Mom would have loved to be there with us. I cried.

This was how my year went. I didn't think about Mom all the time, not even most of the time. Just at those times when I wondered what she would think or when there was something I knew she would have wanted to see. Of course she would have wanted to see everything, every moment of our lives, but she also would not have wanted me to cry too much. She would have told me to be strong, that people die and life goes on.

I know that life goes on. I also know that it is important to mourn, but even mourning has its limits and boundaries. After the Second Temple was destroyed the rabbis debated as to what degree to mourn over the tragedy. Some suggested prohibiting the consumption of meat and wine, but were overruled by the majority who decided that mourning must not be excessive, for people will not be able to bear it. Instead, they ruled:

A man may stucco his house, but he should leave a little bare.

A man can prepare a full-course banquet, but he should leave out an item or two. A woman can put on all her ornaments, but leave off one or two.

The key to healthy mourning is balance. During the *Shiva* the balance is heavily weighted towards mourning. Regular activities are prohibited to ensure its supremacy. During *Shloshim* the balance is closer to even. After *Shloshim*, mourning gradually diminishes until it becomes a tiny, yet significant, part of the balance.

Towards the end of my year, I could sit through a family meal or look at a family photo without actively fighting back tears. I still felt a slight pang of sadness, but I suspect I might feel that for years to come. There are a few things that still bring me to the brink of tears, like watching Mom walk me down the aisle on my wedding video or talking about her last words to me, but I feel that with time, that too will change. There was only one more thing that I feared I would not be able to handle without breaking down.

CHAPTER 15

BRIS

We were due to have a baby boy in a few weeks. Yes, we knew what we were having. We didn't feel the need to be surprised. If the doctor knows, why shouldn't we? When Natalie first informed me about the pregnancy I was sure that it had to be a girl. It would be perfect. We would name her after Mom. She would be a living memorial, the girl that Mom always wanted. When we found out we were having a boy, and my carefully laid out plans were trashed, I was overjoyed. Perhaps it was my chauvinistic side coming out, but what guy doesn't want a son?

The first few weeks after I found out we were having a baby were hard. Thinking about it brought me to tears. Talking about it was nearly impossible. Luckily, we decided to keep it a secret, even from our parents, for the first month or so.

Telling Dad should have been one of the happiest things I've ever had to do. We came to visit on a Sunday. Natalie kept looking at me, prodding me to tell him. It was my job. He was my father. I wanted more than anything to tell him the news, but when I imagined saying the words I was overwhelmed by that feeling you get right before crying. I was afraid to say the words.

I didn't want to cry in front of him, and turn a joyous occasion into a sad one. If he saw me crying it might make him cry. I didn't want to do that. But he was my father and it was my duty. I gathered all my strength, took some deep breaths, tried to distract my mind. This was happy news, a time to celebrate, no reason for tears, just laughter and joy. Natalie said, "Dad, we have some news to tell you," and turned it over to me. I don't remember if I managed to get any words out. I think Natalie actually told him. All I remember is bursting into tears and running upstairs to cry my heart out.

The next few weeks of telling people the news was tough on my emotions, but then it was ok. It was like I had washed the sadness out of my system, or maybe just exhausted it, and could finally enjoy spreading the wonderful news.

The next challenge I had to face was the birth. I didn't think there was any way I'd be able to make it through the labor and birth at Natalie's side in the delivery room. I imagined myself being a total emotional, tear soaked mess. I ended up doing pretty well, just a few quiet tears when I held my son for the first time. It was May 10, 2010 at 9:18pm, exactly ten months since Mom's passing.

Now there was only one more hurdle I had to clear: the *Bris*. In the bible, God commands Abraham to circumcise himself to create a covenant, or *Bris*, between himself and God. God also commands every father to circumcise his son on the eighth day after birth. For the last few thousand years Jewish fathers have fulfilled this commandment, usually through the services of a *Mohel*, a professional circumciser. I wouldn't have to actually do the cutting, but I would have to do something that was, for me, far more daunting: speak.

Jerry Seinfeld points out that the number one fear for most Americans is public speaking. Number two is death. Therefore, given the choice, most people at a funeral would rather be in the coffin than on the podium delivering the eulogy.

Public speaking was not what I was afraid of. I've spoken before my congregation on many occasions and delivered lectures to large audiences. I simply didn't think I'd be able to get through the speech without breaking down. It's one thing to cry in front of your wife and father. Crying in front of an entire audience is a whole different experience. I've seen men do it and it's extremely touching, but not a scene I was particularly interested in replicating. But I had no choice. I was the father. Natalie did her job, and now it was my turn. I had been thinking about what to say since the day we found out we were having a boy. I never got through more than a few sentences in my mind before the tears began welling up. I had no idea how I was going to get through the real thing.

On Tuesday, May 18th, eight days after his birth, we brought our baby boy into the Covenant of Abraham and named him Yehuda Elimelech after Mom, Yehudit daughter of Elimelech. About seventy relatives and friends celebrated with us. I broke down several times, but managed to get through my speech. Here's what I said:

Psalm 116 - "How can I repay God for all His goodness to me? I will lift up the cup of salvation and call on the name of the God. I will fulfill my vows to the God in the presence of all His people. Grievous in the Lord's sight is the death of His devoted ones."

I've recited these verses thousands of times, but I never understood the juxtaposition of giving thanks and death. How can they coexist in the same paragraph? I never understood, until this day, when I say Kaddish and mourn for my mother while welcoming my new son, born exactly ten months after her passing. How can these two extreme opposites, death and thanksgiving, coexist without causing intense emotional and psychological damage? The answer lies in the very next verse of the Psalm – "Please God, for I am Your servant, the son of your maidservant. You release me from my chains." The answer is that there is no answer. We are servants. All we can do is accept our fate and destiny, and move forward.

According to our mystical tradition, the birth of a son during the year of mourning provides tremendous comfort to the soul of the deceased as well as to the family. My son, you have done both. You have given us reason to laugh and rejoice again, and by carrying her name, you will continue to provide comfort and an elevation for your grandmother's soul.

Yehuda and Elimelech are both names of Malchut, kingship, and we will settle for nothing less...(no doctor or lawyer...we're going for the top!) Son, I'd like to tell you a little about the people you are named after.

I remember my grandfather, Elimelech Rajner, as a strong and proud man. When the Nazis entered Warsaw in 1939, he took his wife and baby daughter and fled to Uzbekistan, where he later joined the Polish People's Army to fight the Nazis. He earned a medal for valor in combat and rose to the rank of officer in an army permeated with anti-Semitism. He was always proud of being Jewish and never backed down in the face of persecution. I'll tell you one story that I heard from Mom. In her school, in post war Poland, she had a male teacher who was overtly anti-Semitic to her and persecuted her in class. When her father heard of this he marched into that classroom, grabbed the teacher and lifted him up by his lapels, and threatened to kill him if he ever as much as looked at Mom the wrong way. That was the last time that he, or any other teacher, dared to mess with the daughter of that Jew. Yehuda Elimelech, we hope you will have that same pride and strength to always stand up for your people.

Your grandmother, Yehudit – Jeane Singer – what can I say... She was full of energy, the center of attention, the life of the party. Whatever she did, be it work or play, she did with passion and intensity. But her main passion and goal in life was taking care of her family. She was a 24/7 wife and mother, and would have been a full time, full service grandma. She would have carried your picture around and showed it to everyone who crossed her path. My grandson.

the king. The heavens are shaking, turned upside down, with sounds of rejoicing. Yehudit Bat Elimelech has a grandson, Yehuda Elimelech, and everyone must join in the celebration! May you be blessed with that passion and energy, to accomplish great things in your life, and may you be a blessing and elevation for your grandmother's soul.

Yehuda Elimelech, the greatest blessing that has been bestowed upon you is the same one I have been granted...your Mom, my wife. She is love, kindness, chesed, caring. She has given her unconditional love to me and to my parents, and has been a comfort to us in our darkest hour, and now she is showering that love and kindness on you, her son. I can't think of anyone I would rather have as your Mommy, and my wife. I cannot properly express the gratitude I feel for having her in my life. I, we, are truly blessed.

My son, I will end off with a promise and a blessing. I will teach you and raise you in the ways of our Torah, and always be there to protect you and care for you.

"May God bless you and keep you.
May God cause the divine light to shine upon you
and be gracious to you.
May God turn His face toward you, and grant you
peace."

I'm sad that Mom didn't live to see her grandson. I'm sadder that Yehuda will never get the chance to know his grandmother. He would have learned so much from her, and been treated like a prince, probably spoiled rotten, but in a good way, like his dad. Mom would have wanted us to rejoice, just as, I know, she was looking down upon us and rejoicing, so we did. We celebrated the birth of our son. We celebrated life.

CHAPTER 16

MEMORIES

On one of our visits to Dad's house, I looked through Mom's bedroom drawers. I found old photos of her as a child in Poland, her parents, grandparents, and of course, yours truly. In the night stand next to her bed I found an envelope containing a first place certificate presented to Arnold Singer in 1969 for winning the Belmar, NJ municipal talent show.

Let me explain. For several years of my early childhood my parents rented an apartment for the summer in the quaint, Jersey Shore town of Belmar. Mom loved the beach and the sun, and she loved tanning. She had a darker complexion to begin with, but after a few sessions in the sun, she got really dark, and happy. We had good times during those summers in Belmar.

Mom discovered that the Belmar municipality sponsored an annual talent show in their boardwalk pavilion. I was three years old, bronzed by the sun, with curly locks of blonde hair. All I remember is getting up on a podium and singing *Que Sera Sera*, acapella, complete with hand motions. I think I might have also sung something from *Fiddler on the Roof*, either *Sunrise Sunset* or *If I Were a Rich Man*. Mom was probably the only one who remembered. I must have done well, because I won first prize! I seem to remember Mom coaching and rehearsing with me. She wasn't gonna let her son get up and make a fool of himself in front of the whole town of Belmar! I also vaguely remember doing ad hoc performances at the Russian Tea Room, a famous celebrity hangout near Carnegie Hall in Manhattan. God bless her, she believed in me. She never stopped believing in me. She really thought I had talent, and I guess I did, and maybe still do. She always thought I could be a great writer. To her I was always the best. If only I had the same confidence in my abilities, maybe I would have been a great writer. Maybe I still will.

Along with the photos I also found a cassette tape of my grandmother reciting poetry that Mom recorded not long before grandma's death. Natalie, Dad, and I listened as Grandma recited poems in Polish, Russian, and French. It felt as if she was there in the room with us. It made me wish that I would have recorded my last conversations with Mom. How I would love to hear her voice again, her final words to me. We never think of these things until it's too late.

If I only had another few moments with Mom. There are so many things I want to say, so many questions I want to ask. We've all heard people say this; if only I had a few more minutes. For many of us, it's too late, but if it's not too late for you, then don't wait. Make a list of things you want to know and say. Ask those questions and have those conversations, while you still can. Someday it will be too late, and you'll forever regret missing your chance.

CHAPTER 17

MORTALITY

Before Mom's death, I never seriously thought about dying. Death was something that happened to other people. I would live forever. As my year of mourning drew near to completion I began to think about my own mortality. This new state of mind was probably connected to the birth of my son. Would I live to see him grow up, go to college, marry? Would I ever be a grandfather? I found myself doing the same calculations over and over in my head. I was 44 when Yehuda was born, so I'll be 57 at his Bar Mitzvah. When I'm 72, he'll be 28. Maybe he'll get married early, and have kids right away? I hope he won't wait as long as his dad did.

It pains me to think that I might not live long enough to see my son grow up. Then again, my Dad's mom lived to 102. Who's to say I won't live past 100 and see great grandchildren? This entire exercise is terrifying, depressing, and absolutely frustrating. It's enough to drive you mad! So what do I do when my mind starts plugging numbers into a mental longevity spreadsheet? I remind myself that we each have a mission in this world, a destiny that we have no control over. When that mission is accomplished we die, not a moment sooner or later, regardless of where we are and what we do. Worrying about when that will be is useless.

There's a story of a woman who was diagnosed with a terminal form of cancer, who came to seek the assistance of a visiting Tibetan Lama known for his miraculous healings. Upon seeing the holy man, the woman broke into tears and cried, "I'm going to die." The Lama chuckled goodheartedly and responded, "we are all going to die."

When you accept death, you can live life without fearing it or worrying about it. This doesn't mean that you should not pray for health and long life, eat properly, exercise, and be aware of your safety. You should absolutely do all of these things. I do. It just means that you should make every moment of your life meaningful, and not live in constant fear of the inevitable.

So will I live to see Yehuda grow old? Only God can answer that. For now, I cherish every moment that I have to play with him, hold him, and look into his eyes (and change his diapers, sometimes). Please God, give me the chance to see him become a man, have a family, and grow old.

CHAPTER 18

UNVEILING

Eleven months had passed since Mom's passing and my last day of *Kaddish* was upon me. It was on that Sunday, May 30th, the day before Mom's Hebrew birthday and two days after her secular one, that we chose to dedicate her monument in a ceremony commonly known as the "unveiling".

Judaism obligates that a monument be erected at the head of the grave, to indicate the location of the grave and to assure that the memory of the deceased is not forgotten. The earliest source for this is found in the biblical verse in Genesis, "*And Rachel died and was buried on the way to Ephrat, which is Bethlehem. And Jacob erected a monument on Rachel's grave.*" The "unveiling" is the dedication of that monument.

The monument should be erected as soon after burial as possible, but the dedication can take place up to a year after burial. The custom of placing a veil over the monument and then removing it is not mandated by Jewish tradition, although it has taken hold in America in recent years.

The monument can be any shape or size. The inscription should be engraved into the stone and should contain the complete Hebrew and English name of the deceased, the Hebrew and English dates of birth and death, a brief epitaph such as "beloved wife, mother, grandmother" and the five Hebrew letters that represent the words, "May his (or her) soul be bound in the bond of eternal life." The monument should contain no human or animal images, or photos of the deceased. Jewish symbols such as the Star of David, *Menorah*, or hands forming the priestly benediction sign (for a Kohen) are permissible.

I had briefly considered speaking at the unveiling, but decided to leave that honor to Rabbi Wildes. Standing before Mom's grave was simply too much for me to handle, and I knew there was absolutely no way I would be able to speak coherently without breaking down. Some people are able to speak, even at a parent's funeral, certainly at the unveiling. I'm not one of them. I will have to pay my respects in writing.

There was one thing that I hoped I would be able do to honor Mom with at the unveiling: recite the *El Maleh Rahamim* prayer. I wasn't sure if I would actually go through with it, but it was my plan. The family gathered at the cemetery and walked to the grave. The monument stood at its head. As the rabbi spoke about the legacy that Mom left behind, which we were living, I reflected on the past year. I had done everything I could to honor Mom in the ways of our tradition. I made sure she had a proper Jewish burial. I recited *Kaddish* for her every day. I studied hundreds of pages of Torah in her memory. I performed good deeds and gave charity in her honor. Finally, and most importantly, I named my first son, her first grandson, after her so that she would live on through him and never be forgotten. I will teach Yehuda to be a good person, a good Jew, and to carry his grandmother's name and legacy with pride. Every time I look at him I will remember the kind of parent Mom was, and try to emulate her selflessness and love. I had done everything I possibly could to honor her. I was at peace with myself and I believed that she was grateful for all that I had done to ease her journey and elevate her soul. I was sad that she was gone, but the grief and pain was no longer with me. I felt healed.

When the time came to recite the *El Maleh Rahamim* the rabbi looked at me inquisitively, and I nodded and began chanting the prayer. My voice shook a bit at some parts, but I chanted it sweetly and soulfully, just like Mom would have wanted me to.

El Maleh Rahamin – *God, full of compassion, who dwells on high,*

Grant proper rest on the wings of the divine Presence,

Among the lofty holy and pure who shine like the radiance of heaven,

To the soul of Yehudit daughter of Elimelech who has gone to her eternal destiny, (for I pledge to give charity in her memory),

May her eternal repose be in the Garden of Eden.

Therefore, Master of Compassion, shelter her in Your wings forever,

And bind her in the bond of everlasting life.
The Lord is her inheritance. May she rest in peace,

And let us say, Amen.

Goodbye, Mom. I will never forget you.

EPILOGUE

One of the greatest gifts given to Man is the ability to forget. Without it we would be forever overwhelmed by the pain and grief of our past. Time helps us forget, and as the saying goes, heals all wounds.

Several months have passed since I completed my year of mourning, and I find myself focusing less on Mom's death and more on her life. When I view her photos I think of the beautiful, vibrant, ambitious woman who conquered the world in her own special way. I think of all the happiness and love we shared. I am sad that she cannot enjoy the family that she loved so dearly, but I am comforted knowing that she is looking down upon us with pride and rejoicing. Each time I look at my son's smiling face and into his sparkling eyes I remember the unconditional love she showered upon me, and vow to do the same for him. This is her legacy. She will live on in my heart and in my soul forever.

GLOSSARY

Aninut – see Onen.

Bar Mitzvah – The milestone marking the age of maturity according to Jewish law for a boy, which takes place on his 13th birthday.

Bris – Ritual circumcision.

Chevra Kadisha - "the holy fraternity". The organization responsible for caring for and preparing the corpse for Jewish burial.

Gehinnom – Jewish version of Hell. The name derives from "Gay Ben Hinnom – the Valley of Hinnom" which is located outside the old city walls of Jerusalem and where pagans sacrificed children to the fires of the idol Molech.

Kaddish – A prayer, composed in Aramaic, recited by mourners.

Kabbalat Shabbat – The prayer service recited on Friday evenings to welcome the Sabbath. In most congregations parts of the service are sung.

Keriah - The ritual tearing of the mourner's garment, representing the anguish of the mourner and the irreversibility of death. The torn garment is worn throughout the initial seven day mourning period.

Lecha Dodi – The main prayer/song of the Kabbalat Shabbat service, composed by Rabbi Shlomo Alkebetz in the 16th century in the town of Safed, Israel. The prayer is laced with mystical meanings and references.

Mazel – Luck or good fortune.

Mikvah – Pool of water used for ritual purification.

Minyan – A quorum of ten adult Jewish males required for the recitation of Kaddish and other prayers.

Mitzvot – Commandments and deeds mandated by the Torah and defined by rabbinic law.

Onen – The status of a mourner between the death and burial of one of his or her parent, child, spouse, or sibling.

Petira – Hebrew word for death. It literally means "release".

Rebbe – A Chassidic rabbinic leader.

Rosh Hashanah – The Jewish New Year which is also considered to be the annual Day of Judgment for the entire world. Rosh Hashanah is observed for 2 days and usually falls in September.

Shabbat – The Jewish Sabbath, which begins at sundown on Friday and ends at nightfall on Saturday. It is a day of introspection and prayer, during which families and friends join together to share festive meals and to socialize. According to Jewish law all creative activity is prohibited. Prohibited activities include lighting a flame, cooking, conducting business, writing, driving, using computers or phones, turning lights on or off.

Shofar – A rams horn blown on Rosh Hashana, the Jewish New Year. The shofar represents the ram that God told Abraham to sacrifice instead of Isaac, and therefore is meant to evoke God's compassion in reward for Abraham's willingness to sacrifice for Him.

Shteible – Yiddish term for a small synagogue usually located in a private home.

Tachrichin - (Takh-ree-kheen), the traditional clean, unadorned, white, handmade linen shrouds that a Jewish corpse is clothed in for burial. These shrouds symbolize purity, simplicity, and dignity. They have no pockets, to represent the futility of material possessions in the eternal world of the spirit.

Tahara – Literally, purification. The process of cleansing and preparing a Jewish corpse for burial.

Yom Kippur – The Day of Atonement during which is also a day of fasting that begins in the evening and lasts for slightly over 24 hours.

Neshama - Soul

Mishnah – The series of volumes containing the Oral Law passed from God to Moses from generation to generation.

Talmud – The expansion and explanation of the Mishnah.

Yeshiva – Academy of Jewish learning or a Jewish day school.

PRACTICAL GUIDE TO JEWISH MOURNING

The following guide is a brief overview of the Jewish customs and tradition related to death and mourning. All of the listed customs and traditions are discussed in the book. There are also many wonderful resources on the internet, and in books, that deal with the specifics of Jewish law and tradition relating to mourning in great detail. Specific questions regarding any of the points mentioned below can be directed to your rabbi or to the author.

Initial Care of the Deceased

1. Open a window. Close the eyes and mouth of the deceased.

2. Call your rabbi. If you don't have one, the funeral home will have rabbis that they can call to conduct the funeral.

3. Call a Jewish funeral home to arrange for the body to be cared for. The body of a deceased Jew should only be touched and handled by Jews. A funeral director of a traditional Jewish funeral home will be aware of this. In the event that there are no Jewish funeral home personnel available, you will need to assist

in lifting the body onto a stretcher for transport.

4.   The funeral director will arrange for members of the Chevra Kaddisha (burial society) to perform the Tahara and prepare the body for burial.

5.   If the deceased does not own a burial plot, you must purchase one. The funeral director or your rabbi will be able to help if needed.

6.   The funeral and burial must take place as soon after death as possible, preferably the same day.

7.   The funeral and burial may not take place on the Sabbath or Jewish holidays when work is prohibited.

8.   There should always be a Jewish shomer with the body. The shomer should recite psalms.

9.   Jewish tradition requires that the casket be made of wood and unadorned. The simpler the casket, the better.

Funeral

1.   Mourners include a mother, father, husband, wife, son, daughter, brother, and sister.

2.   Before the funeral the rabbi will perform Keriya, tearing the outer garment of the mourner, while the mourner recites the blessing:

Baruch Atah Adonoy Eloheynu Melech Haolom Dayan Ha-emet.

Blessed are you Lord our God, King of the universe, the True Judge.

3. The rabbi recites psalms and delivers a eulogy. Other eulogies may also be delivered.

4. The casket is lifted by pallbearers and carried out to the hearse. The mourners and the congregation follow the casket. Psalm 91 is recited.

Burial

1. The casket is carried to the grave while Psalm 91 is recited. The procession pauses seven times (except on Friday after midday or on holidays when burial is permitted).

2. The rabbi speaks briefly.

3. The casket is lowered into the grave.

4. The mourners throw the first clump of earth onto the casket, using the back of a shovel. The shovel is then left in the ground for the next person to take it. It is a great sign of respect for the deceased for the grave to be completely filled in by those attending the burial.

5. When the grave is entirely covered with earth, the mourners recite the Kaddish.

6. The Tziduk Hadin prayer is recited (except on Friday after midday or on holidays when burial is permitted).

7. Two lines are formed between which the mourners pass. As the mourners pass, those forming the line recite the traditional prayer of consolation:

Hamakom Yenachem Eschem Btoch Shar Aveiley Tzion V'Yerushalyim.

May the Omnipresent console you among the other mourners of Zion and Jerusalem.

8. It is customary to wash ones hands upon leaving the cemetery.

9. A monument is erected at the head of the grave at any time during the year after burial.

Shiva

1. Shiva begins after the burial.

2. The mourners spend seven days in a home.

3. All mirrors in the home should be covered.

4. A seven day candle remains lit throughout the Shiva.

5. The mourners sit on the floor or on low stools and wear the garment torn at the funeral.

6. People visit the mourners to console them. They recite the traditional consolation prayer.

7. Mourners may not wear leather shoes, bathe for pleasure, anoint themselves with oil or perfume, shave or get a haircut, engage in marital relations, and study Torah.

8. All entertainment is prohibited.

9. Mourners should not work or leave the house if possible.

10. Prayer services are held at the Shiva home. A mourner should lead services if possible.

11. The mourners recite Kaddish at services.

12. Mourners may attend synagogue on the Sabbath. All public displays of mourning are suspended. The shiva continues after the Sabbath.

13. Jewish festivals during which work is prohibited cancel the Shiva. For example, if the Shiva begins on a Sunday, and Passover begins on Tuesday, then the Shiva is canceled on Tuesday morning.

Shloshim

1. The thirty day period of mourning encompassing the Shiva.

2. Shaving, haircuts, and live entertainment are prohibited for mourners.

3. Mourners attend synagogue services and recite Kaddish.

4. Mourners may not attend parties or joyous gatherings, including weddings.

Twelve Months

1. The full year of mourning applies only to a son or daughter mourning a parent.

2. Attending joyous gatherings and live entertainment is prohibited.

3.   Kaddish is recited until the end of the eleventh month.

Yahrtzeit, the annual anniversary of the passing, is commemorated by lighting a 24 hour candle and the recitation of Kaddish.

Mourner's Kaddish
Transliterated

Yis-gadal v'yis-kadash sh'may raba,

B'alma dee-v'ra chee-ru-say, ve'yam-lich mal-chusay,

B'chai-yay-chon uv'yo-may-chon uv-cha-yay d'chol beis Yisrael,

Ba-agala u'vizman ka-riv, ve'imru, **Amen.**

Y'hay sh'may raba me'varach le-alam uleh-almay alma-ya.

Yis-barach v'yish-tabach, v'yis-pa-ar v'yis-romam v'yis-nasay,

V'yis-hadar v'yis-aleh v'yis-halal sh'may d'koo-d'shah,

B'rich hu.

L'ayla meen kol beer-chasa v'shee-rasa,

Toosh-b'chasa v'nay-ch'masa, da-a meeran b'alma, ve'imru

Amen.

Y'hay sh'lama raba meen sh'maya v'chayim aleynu

V'al kol Yisrael, ve'imru, **Amen.**

O'seh shalom beem-romav, hoo ya'ah-seh shalom aleynu

V'al kol Yisrael, ve'imru, **Amen.**

ADDITIONAL INFORMATION

Find additional photos, updates, and changes at:

http://www.citronpublishing.com/goodbyemom

For additional information on Jewish prayer and mourning:
http://www.myjewishguide.com

Contact Arnie Singer at: arnie.singer@gmail.com

For bulk purchases: http://www.citronpublishing.com

14319221R00121

Made in the USA
Lexington, KY
22 March 2012